Carving Hope Out Of Depression

Carving Hope Out Of Depression

Victory Over Darkness and a Path to Self-Love

DAVID HARDER

Scripture quotations marked (NKJ) and scripture taken from the New King James Version®. Copyright © 1982 by Thomas Nelson, Inc. Used by permission. All rights reserved.

Scripture quotations marked (NLT) are taken from the Holy Bible, New Living Translation, copyright © 1996, 2004, 2007 by Tyndale House Foundation. Used by permission of Tyndale House Publishers, Inc., Carol Stream, Illinois 60188. All rights reserved.

All Scripture quotations marked (GNT) and scripture in this publication are taken from the Good News Translation® in Today's English Version – Second Edition, Copyright © 1992 American Bible Society. Used by Permission.

Drawbaugh Publishing Group
444 Allen Drive
Chambersburg PA 17202

Book ISBN: 978-1-941746-00-4
eBook ISBN: 978-1-941746-01-1

For Worldwide Distribution, Printed in the United States.

1 2 3 4 5 6 7 8 9 10 / 20 19 18 17 16 15 14

"Second Chances – A Cry from the Heart"

A poem by Kim Moore and used with permission[1]

– – –

I wish that I could lie, like the sand,
and let the warm ocean waves wash over me,
Removing all the things that don't belong in my life,
And when it's finished, let the sun dry my tears
and bleach my heart pure and white.
If only I could stand on a mountaintop
and look at the perfect world below,
Without the trace of war and death, poverty
and hunger, disappointment and sadness,
Breathe in fresh, pure air and watch as eagles soar
freely in the blue sky above.
To float weightlessly in the depths of the ocean,
where silence engulfs the angry voices
of those who dwell on land,
Watching, as light moves, and changes colors and shapes,
while dancing with brightly colored beings whose water is home,
Lovingly surrounded, like a baby in the womb,
not yet knowing the worry and cares of life,
I yearn to fly high above the clouds
where only the sound of the wind whispers in my ear
and the soft brilliance of the clouds
reflect their perfection.
Where concern is carried faraway, in an instant,

and the rush of beauty is all around,
The earth, with all its problems and pain,
faraway beneath the clouds and out of sight,
To have the chance to start again
and do it all right – the way it should have been.
A second chance at life, a second chance to live,
a second chance to make the choices
I should have made back then.
And what would I do with a second chance?
Would I see the light, hear wisdom spoken,
or run back to the choices
that have pulled me into this darkness?
I did not listen then; I ran away,
choosing everything that has brought me
down—and left standing—alone—in this hell I've made.

Table Of Contents

Foreword

If you ever wanted to find the answers and causes for your depression, and how to overcome the feelings, then *Carving Hope Out Of Depression* is the book for you. Written by a layman, David Harder unashamedly bares his soul detailing his journey from years of failure to a life enriched with hope. Using practical language, David explains the steps necessary to achieve freedom and peace from the debilitating affect of depression. David realized his wrong choices were at fault and he quickly discovered that it wasn't God who was the source of his punishment.

Our words either set us free or set us in bondage. Words are powerful, including the words we tell ourselves. When we speak words of self-condemnation, our oppression intensifies isolating us from friends and loved ones. Too often, we think God is out to destroy or hurt us, but the opposite is true. While we are bogged down in depression, God is quietly trying to pull us free, keeping us alive so He can bring us to a place of victory. *Carving Hope Out of Depression* is a refreshing book which addresses David's personal journey from hate, mistrust, and loneliness onto a path of light and love.

Thoughts of suicide are not limited to individuals strung out on drugs, someone sitting in jail, or some homeless individual unable to obtain a job or afford food. Members of my own family battle depression and have considered suicide. After reading David's work, I wish his book had been available years earlier. In fact, I intend to purchase copies and distribute them to contacts around the world. I believe David's book will permanently change lives for the better.

In all my years as a minister, I have counseled thousands of individuals who are caught in a web of depression. Tragically, I've watched individuals consider suicide as a way to cope with their condition. Yet, unfortunately, depression is on the rise in our society.

During my years in Florida, I worked with CARP (Comprehensive Alcoholism Rehabilitation Programs) in West Palm Beach. We developed a nine-month rehab program targeting individuals fighting substance abuse. While many of the steps listed in David's book are similar to the methods we taught at CARP, *Carving Hope Out of Depression* delivers practical words, by God, which will bring supernatural healing.

I also believe small groups and church sponsored special interest studies will benefit from David's book. It is time we stop hiding our depression and starting finding reliable answers for our future happiness. I met David when he began attending our church in Lakeside, AZ, but in a very short time, I've come to appreciate David's passion for reaching out to hurting individuals. His desire to help others, who like himself have greatly suffered, I think will eventually lead him to write more books; perhaps even a series of books that will build on the ideas within these pages.

Carving Hope Out of Depression isn't just a feel-good book for church attending individuals. In these pages are wisdom and solutions, including concepts that are easy to understand and apply, that will reach out to all people. This book will enrich your life and quite possibly instill a compassion for those who suffer from depression.

Richard G. Boen
Pastor (The New Living Church),
entrepreneur, patriot, and church pioneer.

Acknowledgements

I would like to thank my Aunt Dorothy, who turns 104 this August 21st, 2014. She has always been an inspiration and mentor for me as she is one of the kindest, sweetest, persons I have ever met. Since her eighties, she has battled the loss of one eye and cataracts, broken and replaced both hips—once during a bowling activity, fell and broke her neck, broke her shoulder, dislocated the other, and through this all, she remains firm in her Godly beliefs and maintains a positive outlook on life. She is an amazing woman and a terrific mother to three gifted adult children—two who are currently living. Despite the loss of hearing, she will engage you in a lively discussion about any modern topic or current event and will run circles around most contestants on television's *Jeopardy* show. Thank you, Aunt Dorothy for your support, inspiration, devotion, and love.

I have a group of friends (Ruth, Jody, Ruthie, Mary, John, Kat, Stephen, Deane, Shelia, Mary, Lynanne, Kim, and Cathy—who went home to be with the Lord recently) that have been a source of strength for me during difficult times while writing this book. Thank you for listening and encouraging me.

The love of my life and my partner is Emily. She is my leading fan, an excellent critic, and the most significant person in my life. For us to even meet each other, it took me 61 years and divine intervention.

There is a host of friends who have had the opportunity to pre-read this book and have encouraged me to press forward and not quit. I could not have accomplished writing this book without their kindness and support. I am thankful for their encouragement.

In a special word of gratitude, I cannot thank the editor of my book enough. Cori Linder (http://twitter.com/editorcori) was an instrumental player in seeing my manuscript transformed into a success and a published book. Her technical expertise exceeded my expectations allowing me to produce a manuscript filled with inspiration. She is fantastic at what she does best; assisting writers to be great authors. Thank you from the bottom of my heart.

Also, I wish to thank my publisher, Dean Drawbaugh of Drawbaugh Publishing Group. Dean's insight and direction for my book provided me with the perspective necessary to see this book delivered to a broad audience. He not only understood my reasons for writing my book, but additionally he provided the guidance to see this project to the finished end. Thank you for your commitment to my story.

Finally, but most importantly, I wish to thank God for being patient with me despite the various detours I've taken in my life. You alone laid out plans for my life, ones that I wasn't aware of, nor did I heed for many years. But, by the grace of God I am what I am and shall serve You, the One who loved me long before I was born. To God be the glory forever, and ever. Amen.

Introduction to the Subject of Depression

This material was obtained and written by Joseph M. Carver, Ph.D., a psychologist in private practice at Joseph M. Carver, Ph.D., Inc. in Portsmouth, Ohio.[2] It is printed here with permission.

Depression is perhaps the most common of all mental health problems, currently felt to affect one in every four adults to some degree. Depression is a problem with mood or feeling in which the mood is described as sad, feeling down in the dumps, being blue, or feeling low. While the depressed mood is present, evidence is also present which reflects the neurochemical or "brain chemistry" aspects of depression with the depressed individual experiencing poor concentration or attention, loss of energy, accelerated thought and worry, sleep or appetite disturbance, and other physical manifestations. When this diagnosis is present, the individual will display at least five of the following symptoms during the depressive periods:

- Depressed mood, most of the day or every day
- Markedly diminished interest in all or almost all activities
- Significant weight loss or gain or appetite disturbance
- Insomnia or excessive sleeping
- Psychomotor agitation or retardation (restlessness)
- Low energy level or severe tiredness
- Feelings of inadequacy, loss of self-esteem, and/or self-deprecation
- Decreased attention, concentration, or ability to think clearly
- Recurrent thoughts of death or suicide, an expressed desire to be dead

Prologue

An Introduction

It was August 2012, and I was at the end of my rope and seriously depressed. Faith in anything ceased to exist. Life had no meaning, and I felt as if religion failed me. The news media weren't helping me either.

It's impossible to listen to the radio or watch television and not be bombarded with daily news reports of mass murders or about individuals who take guns and start shooting people in malls, theaters, at work, and in schools. Throughout the world, there are wars and conflicts ravaging nations.

Watching and listening to these reports, we delude ourselves into thinking it can't happen to our friends, our family, or us. Yet, the unsettling likelihood exists that you or someone you know has been a victim or died of a serious crime.

Unemployment rates have remained high for years, and according to CNSnews.com (reported on February 3, 2012) there are 44.7 million Americans receiving food stamps.[3] The cost of living continues to rise faster than our ability to earn, and the amount of homeless people is at an all-time high. The number of criminals imprisoned exceeds the capacity of the systems meant to house them. According to the National Institute of Drug Abuse, 22.5 million Americans have used illicit drugs or abused psychotherapeutic medications.[4] Their research shows the number is increasing by almost 5% each year. The website CDC.gov points out that marriage continues to end in divorce at a rate just under 50%.[5]

We are blasted with negative news and information daily influencing the feelings of depression or hopelessness that will strike nearly everyone at some point and time in their life. We are struggling to live, eat, and survive. When it comes to the feelings of depression—illness, death of a friend or family member, loss of a job or mate, and sacrifice of a home through foreclosure—these represent just the tip of the iceberg. The list of causes could go on forever. Is it any wonder why we feel hopeless about certain aspects of life?

Some people shrug the effects. Others learn to cope with life's pressures with drugs and alcohol, and some individuals will turn to a spiritual institution. Sometimes, certain individuals can't cope and will resort to violence leading to mass killings and shooting sprees. We want answers, the reasons why, yet we feel the pain of depression inside our head and know it's real.

In our journey to conquer depression, I can assure you, this book may not provide the absolute answers you're seeking, but it will supply you with the answers that worked for me. I'll share the problems I faced, and the insights I discovered. More importantly, I will show you where you can search for the answers and how you can find hope in the process. This book is for you if you have experienced or struggled with any or all the following:

- You're considering suicide because you can't cope
- Your life seems empty and meaningless
- Drugs, alcohol, or prescription medication allow you to cope with life
- You're confused, or feel hopeless about your future
- You want to know why some turn to God in uncertain times
- You think there is more to life than what you're experiencing now
- You can't resolve science and what the church teaches about creation
- You belong to one faith, and despise the "others"
- Your thought of being a "good person" is the right answer to the challenges facing humanity
- You can't understand how a "just" God would allow the world to get where it is today

- You're incarcerated in prison, hate your circumstances, and want to be free
- You grew up in some religious setting or home, and your life is miserable
- You think you're tough and can handle any situation
- At one time, you were a religious person, but now you're struggling with the principles
- Everyone views you as smiling on the outside but inside you're hurting

At first, it may seem that I wrote this book for everyone. Well, you're correct because like you, I've identified with many of the above statements. I was searching for answers, but only recently discovered them. It wasn't the whole truth, but I opened the door, which lead me to the next door, and then the next. A journey that started long ago, interrupted, began again, sidetracked, and finally I was shown a glimpse of the truth I had missed along the way.

I share my journey in hopes you won't give up. I was depressed, felt hopeless, and near the final act of taking my own life. I no longer could smile and pretend everything was okay, yet no one knew my depression was pushing me to the brink. For me, suicide was the answer, an end to my emotional pain, and I convinced myself that no one would care. However, I discovered I was wrong. Misguided, I confused death with an end to my pain, but nothing could be further from the truth.

This is why I'm sharing my experiences in this book, hoping like me, you too will find a way to the truth. If you're reading everything up to this point, and are willing to join me on this path of discovery, my wish is that you will continue moving forward on through the next chapters.

You must know I'm not a therapist. I didn't graduate from a theological seminary. I'm just an average person struggling to survive this journey called life. Along the way, I discovered information, which may encourage and help you. To write this book required personal courage, because I've laid bare certain aspects of my life that are far from a stellar performance. Nonetheless, during my journey, I have discovered there are no crimes, wrong deeds, or mistakes that can ever separate us from the most powerful love in the universe.

Reviewing this Chapter

Are you now, or have you ever been depressed?

_____

_____

_____

_____

_____

_____

_____

Is hiding your depression from others an answer?

_____

_____

_____

_____

_____

_____

_____

_____

Is your depression triggered by someone or something?

_____

_____

_____

_____

_____

_____

_____

_____

Has the thought of self-death crossed your mind?

_____

_____

_____

_____

_____

_____

_____

_____

Will you team up with me, to overcome your depression?

_____

_____

_____

_____

_____

_____

_____

_____

_____

Chapter 1

Two Things Before We Start

First, be sure to read this entire first chapter of my book. It will only take a few minutes. This is especially critical for those of you who are considering suicide. Please stop; don't do it!

I was near this point myself, but thankfully didn't act on it. If you're feeling suicidal, the following lifeline is available 24 hours a day. Please call, someone will want to speak with you. Here is the telephone number for the National Suicide Prevention Lifeline:

1-800-273-8255

Suicide seems like an answer, a way to escape the pain, and no one gets hurt in the process, except the one who took his or her own life. But, nothing could be further from the truth. Your pain and the loss of your life will affect everyone around you.

Since you didn't hatch out of an egg on your own, it took two people to make you. In addition, probably several others helped to deliver you, feed, clothe, teach, educate, plus work and play with you—so you're not alone as much as you think. When you're gone, you'll leave a mysterious hole in the lives of your family, friends, associates, and even casual acquaintances. The ones you thought would be okay without you will not be able to make sense of your loss. They will carry in their heart a dark hole you will leave for the rest of their lives!

Choose to survive.

Second, I don't care what religion you're affiliated with, I'm asking that you read the following prayer aloud:

> *God, I am asking You to hear these words being read. Send Angels to watch over and protect me. I'm feeling depressed and hopeless, or can't make sense of life, but I am willing to read this book. Help me to understand, and push all preconceived ideas out of my head.*

If you spoke these words with meaning, then terrific. If you're feeling even slightly skeptic, please go back and reread this prayer. In fact, it's okay if you need to read it many times. I need you to remain open-minded as we move forward to the next chapters. By the way, you will find a summary of all the prayers used in this book on page 147.

I need to mention also that what you believe about the world and how it came into existence, is not up for discussion because it lacks importance. If you belong to a church, or affiliate with some organized religious group, this also is not essential right now. You might be Hindu, Buddhist, or Shinto, subscribe to Islam, Judaism, Christianity, or believe in nothing, and yet I assure you, this information although compelling is not significant. When you're depressed and losing hope, nothing matters. But, I promise, there are answers.

What remains crucial is that you stay open-minded and set aside any preconceived ideas about God, Jehovah, Yahweh, Allah, Jesus, and the Bible. I will explain my thoughts on this as we continue. After completing this book, if you decide to hold on to your original beliefs, I cannot judge you. This is your individual choice.

Every human being who ever existed, or is living now, arrived on this planet through choice. It may simply be that two people had sex, and a child was created (on purpose or by accident), but in the end, whether the infant continued life or was aborted, this occurred because of a choice. In the same way, death is about choices. Granted, not all death is a choice because sometimes, genetic flaws or disease will contribute to death, but the rest—wars, murders, accidents, suicide, capital punishment—are all about choice. If you choose to ignore your body's warning signs or seek medical attention when you're sick, and you die, then it was a choice.

We face choices every second of our life. Some options are life changing while others seem insignificant. The decisions we make not only affect our life but all those around us, whether we know them or not. What if Alexander Fleming had given up and chose to quit on life? You say you don't know this person. Well, Mr. Fleming experienced tragedy, setbacks, and failures, yet he discovered penicillin. A single man and his discovery have affected millions of people worldwide.

There are many examples of how this same story plays out, but I believe that you understand my meaning. Since no one can predict the future, you're left with the here and now, this moment in which you choose to take action or not. So, stay open-minded, and let's find the truth together.

Right now, you're deciding whether to close this book or read further; I'm hoping you'll select the later. Remember, your life is a result of your choices.

Reviewing this Chapter

Suicide is a choice. Are you willing to set aside those feelings and journey with me to find hope?

_____

_____

_____

_____

_____

_____

Can you remain open-minded through this journey?

_____

_____

_____

_____

_____

_____

Living and life are options. Do these seem impossible for you?

_____

_____

_____

_____

_____

_____

_____

_____

We cannot predict the future. Are you afraid of what the future will bring?

_____

_____

_____

_____

_____

_____

_____

_____

Life is an accumulation of our choices. Do your choices feel wrong or confusing?

_____

_____

_____

_____

_____

_____

_____

_____

Chapter 2

What is the Meaning of Life?

For answers, I've often turned to the shelves of leading bookstores, which are brimming with terrific self-help books covering a wide range of topics. The goal of these books is to help us become better, understood, more adjusted, and "normal" people. There's only one problem. When you're depressed and losing hope, none of the words on the pages stops the conversations inside your head or halts the negative spiral thinking. The thoughts telling you death is the answer.

Don't get me wrong. I have plenty of these books sitting on my shelves, and I've even read them cover to cover. Some are fantastic books, which help a person solve issues. However, when you're feeling lost and hopeless, it becomes an effort just to read. I should mention, if you're lucky enough to afford counseling, or have a priest, pastor, or rabbi to confide in, I urge you to exercise those options immediately. Don't wait. Make the call.

For me, I was desperate and didn't have any of the alternatives I've mentioned. I ended a destructive relationship on grossly negative terms, was out of work, and faced felony misdemeanor charges. I settled the court mess and started what I thought was a new relationship with long-term opportunities; only it abruptly ended without explanation. I was then homeless and slept on a friend's sofa.

Years earlier, I had injured my back requiring complicated surgery, followed by minor surgeries every other year, and taking painkillers to survive. The sofa wasn't helping my situation.

I have been married three times, and in two additional significant relationships, yet I found myself single with nothing to show for my efforts. Clearly, I was a textbook human disaster and the epitome of being in the mucky trenches of life. You might be thinking that I have nothing to complain about; that your story is worse. You may be correct.

The thing is depression and loss of hope can strike any person, making them think they are alone. You may be wealthy, famous, a movie or music star, poor, unemployed, homeless, in prison, or dying of some awful disease; depression and loss of hope can strike, for they don't care about your appearance or status. When you're in that space, your head tells you death is the only option.

It is times like this when people begin to question themselves, or their religion, their friends or family, and even the meaning of life. A vortex of negative thinking consumes their thoughts and disturbs sleep patterns. Hope disappears and soon they find themselves in a foul mood. Work associates, friends, and family start to avoid them. The feeling of being alone devours them, and their options narrow down quickly.

There are those who will tell you life is not fair. In fact, life can be difficult. I used to have a philosophy that stated: *Life is a series of trials, hardships, and difficult situations, followed by periods of unexpected happiness.* Since starting my journey (one that I hope you'll join me in), I'm finding I need to change my philosophical position.

What is the meaning of life? How did we get here? Where are we going? What's my purpose here? I have struggled for most of my life questioning the meaning of life and my purpose. There are philosophers who also have expounded on these questions for thousands of years. Nearly every religion you can name identifies these statements with someone or something outside the human realm. Plato, Socrates, Buddha, Jesus, Nietzsche, Vonnegut, Goethe, and many others have tried to answer these questions.

Some of man's earliest written texts exist today in the form of the Torah (Hebrew Bible – Old Testament), Koran (Arabic – Teachings of Muhammad), the teachings of Buddha, and Hinduism. Many are several thousand years old stretching some 5,000 years back. Each text or teaching creates an order of conduct for its followers and tries to explain the reasons for life. Last, each teaching explains what will happen if the follower fulfills the instructions written, or their reward.

The problem for me is that no one knows exactly 100% what happens after death, or what's on the other side. Dead people don't talk. Books, movies, clairvoyants, and religious teachers try to explain what they think is the answer, but again there is no proof. Therefore, it all boils down to a belief system.

The oldest religions of Islam, Judaism, and some Native American Indians believe in the existence of God. The other groups have multiple gods or spirits to rely on. Even those who cling to the writings of Charles Darwin as a premise for how we arrived as humans must understand that Darwin did not deny the existence of God.[6]

Science explains that life evolved (which it has but on a small-scale), that random events occurred, and from this chaos developed humans, animals, and all that we see. When the Big-Bang theory was explained to me in college, the professor broke this one event into many subsections. In each of the divisions, he explained that incredible stuff occurred, until finally, the event was finished and most of what we know about the universe and life came into being.

When I asked the professor to estimate the time span between these subsections, he broke them down into parts of a second. I was shocked when he explained the whole event probably took mere seconds. In fact, a recent report by the European Space Agency (by Associated Press, March 21, 2013) says; *"...the universe burst from subatomic size to its now-observable expanse in a fraction of a second."*[7] We combined from tiny particles into the earth and humans in less than a second. Wow!

Further, when I studied anatomy in school, I saw the intricate parts of the human body. The complexities of blood, air, chemistry, and a host of information I didn't fully understand, make up our human body. How could anyone ever study this information and not realize the hand of God is baffling. Our bodies are far too complicated for accidental creation.

The idea that two microscopic organisms—things we cannot see with the naked eye like sperm from a man and the egg from a woman—can join to create another life is astonishing. From this union, cells divide making bones, teeth, nails, muscle, skin, eyes, hair, and a brain. Roughly nine months later, most of the time, another human being enters this world.

I have a difficult time accepting that my two examples are haphazard or by accident. Therefore, I choose to believe in a Godly creation and ignore the concepts of happenstance. Nevertheless, a belief in the existence of God doesn't explain life or its meaning.

Positive motivational thinkers and writers will tell you that life is what you make it, but if you're down-and-out, it's difficult to see things their way. When we look around at our society, the killings, wars, unemployment, earthquakes, and even the meteors falling-out of the sky, it's fair to say a person is going to feel a wee bit negative. So, what's the answer to surviving, and what is the meaning of life?

To understand the meaning of life, you must first be alive, a breathing, functioning, living being. Place your fingers across the vein running along your neck. Do you feel a pulse? If you feel your heart beating on that vein, you qualify as a living being, imperfect, but alive. If you have a life (which we just confirmed you have), you must give it meaning. If not, you're heading in the wrong direction. Even if you're sitting on death row awaiting execution, you must give your life meaning. How, you ask?

The common thread among philosophers and religion is doing unselfish things for your fellow human—a worthy and admirable quality. But, is this enough? To feel that life has meaning, you need to experience self-worth: that your life means something. I daresay that if I told this to someone on death row, I would get an ear full, and in explicit language. No, it takes more than these things. It requires an awareness of God.

Earlier, I asked you to keep an open mind, so please don't slam the door closed just yet. Hear what I have to say first because you have nothing to lose. To understand God, a person has to understand what God is saying about Himself. Don't just take my word for it either, or anyone else for that matter. You must discover this information out for yourself. Just quoting some phrases out of the Bible doesn't make me an expert in theology. I recommend you read this book for yourself and verify what I'm about to share.

The Bible is one of the world's most ancient writings and has the highest number of printed copies of any book written. According to EnglishMajorsUnite.com (July 3, 2012) the Bible is the top most published book in the world with over 3.9 billion copies printed.[8] There are 66 to 81 books in the Bible (depending on the version you accept) written over a 5,000-year period and by 40 or more authors with diverse backgrounds and educations. The Bible is divided into two main sections called the Old and New Testaments. The Old Testament covers the oral to written history of the Hebrews while the New Testament deals with the life of Jesus and his purpose for us. The Bible, also called scriptures, is a book of history, but also as a book dealing with life and understanding God; it also reveals what's going to happen in the future. We can consider the Bible a life-teaching tool.

For example, in the New Testament, Second Timothy 3:16 (Good News Translation – GNT) it says:

> *"All Scripture is inspired by God and is useful for teaching the truth, rebuking error, correcting faults, and giving instruction for right living."*

This is a clear message—the written words of the Bible contain instructions that are God inspired to teach us the truth about life, giving us a path to live a life with meaning. Many of us are familiar with Old Testament laws in the form of the Ten Commandments. Nearly every nation in the world has a societal foundation based on these Ten Commandments, but the Bible is more than this. It is a conduit for communicating with and understanding God.

Equally important, the Bible provides hope. Hope beyond sickness, depression, and even death; hope for meaning to our lives, answers to our questions, and happiness in our existence. I explained earlier that life is all about choices. Sometimes the decisions we make lead to serious results. I'm here to assure you that regardless the choices you've made in the past if you search for God at any point, He will not ignore you. You might laugh at this statement, and ask, *"Even if I'm on death row?"* The answer is yes!

The New Testament records the life of Jesus. He was nailed to a Roman cross as His death punishment.[9] While slowly dying, there were two men on either side of Jesus and receiving the same punishment. One man scoffed at Jesus telling Him that if He were the Son of God,

He should jump down off that cross and save all of them hanging there. The other dying man rebuked the first man telling him to fear God. He further said that they deserved to die for they were criminals, but this Jesus is innocent. Then, according to Luke 23:43 (GNT), the second criminal heard Jesus say to him:

"I promise you that today you will be in Paradise (heaven) with me."

Now, here is a man in the final minutes of his life. He turned to God, wasn't ignored, but he learned the meaning of his life; that he would enter heaven. There was hope for a criminal being executed for his crimes. Why? Because he sought out God, confessed his crimes, and then found hope. The hope and life meaning were always available, but the criminal made other selections earlier in his life, and chose his own path. He finally realized his mistake when his decisions brought him to a cross for punishment. Nonetheless, God gave the man meaning to his life and told him he would go to heaven upon his death and be with Jesus.

The meaning of life may elude us, but it can be found in and through God. There are stories throughout the Bible where people find God and discover meaning for their lives. They find hope, purpose, and sometimes make a deviation in their journey that is opposite to their previous path. They start seeking the truth about life. They make different choices.

If you're ready to start down this path and want to know the truth, to give your life meaning, then join me. I haven't arrived at any destination, but I continue the path to discover the true meaning for my life. If my story is any example, the changes won't happen overnight, but over time, the differences in your life will be obvious. Depression and hopelessness can feel like a prison, but believe me, hope is alive, and it can begin today. When you're ready, read aloud the following prayer:

God, I am asking You to hear these words. Send Angels to watch over and protect me. I feel depressed and hopeless, and can't make sense of life, but I want to know You. Help me to understand the words of the Bible and push all the negative thoughts out of my head.

If you're anything like me—I can be stubborn—read this prayer several times. And, ideally read the words aloud. When you hear the words spoken in your own voice, this prayer has more impact.

This is your first step, and only the beginning of the first door of many that you must figuratively walk through. It is the start of a new journey and one I hope you'll remain committed to fulfilling. You'll see why this step is critical as you read this book's next chapters.

Life is a choice. Now let's find meaning for your life.

Reviewing this Chapter

Do you know exactly 100% what will happen after your death?

_____

_____

_____

_____

_____

_____

Do you believe the world and we humans are an accident?

_____

_____

_____

_____

_____

_____

_____

_____

Is your depression and loss of hope creating desperation for you?

_____

_____

_____

_____

_____

_____

_____

_____

Do you know how to give your life meaning?

_____

_____

_____

_____

_____

_____

_____

_____

Describe your self-worth.

_____

_____

_____

_____

_____

_____

_____

_____

_____

Have you ever read the Bible to discover God?

_____

_____

_____

_____

_____

_____

_____

_____

_____

Do you feel your situation is so dire; there is no possibility of hope?

_____

_____

_____

_____

_____

_____

_____

_____

_____

Chapter 3

Nothing Happened

The troubles in my life were briefly introduced earlier, but to explain my transformation, from being-intent-on-suicide to my current journey, it's necessary I share more details about my past. Like some of you, I can say that my family background was odd at best.

My father was 11 years older than my mother was and they eloped when my mother turned 18. As an adult, when I think about a nearly 30-year-old man sweeping an 18-year-old high schoolgirl off the street to marry, I experience a chill down my spine. Yet, these were my parents. This is when my story becomes further complicated.

Dad was the youngest of 11 children. His father passed away when my dad was nine because his father's Model-A Ford stalled on the tracks of an oncoming railroad train. With most of his older brothers married and gone, dad was raised by his widowed mother and a few older sisters. They were strict German Mennonites, and religious fervor played a prominent role in his upbringing, especially the part about *sparing the rod spoils the child*. I feel they played this part too well.

At some point early in my dad's adult life, he became addicted to barbiturates. He obtained the drugs through his doctors and continued using them until his death at 88. Living with the substance abuse, I'm amazed he lived so long. My father (and my mother afterward) claimed the barbiturates were prescribed for stomach ailments that plagued my father. As children growing up in this environment, my sisters, brother, and I had no idea of our father's habit but felt the aftermath of his addiction. Dad could be kind and speak loving words in one breath, then launch into being a raging tyrant the next. We had no idea what triggered him or what would set him off. Mother and we children lived in constant fear. When he was upset, my father could be abusive mentally, emotionally, and physically. He was strong and favored a heavy leather belt over a bare butt for his punishment sessions.

It was an emotional rollercoaster, and I became a pleaser to avoid conflict. Until I sought counseling for this issue at age 40, whenever a male authority figure raised his voice and began to yell at me, I would shut down inside, cowering in fear. I still sometimes fight those urges, but I now feel healthier and better equipped to handle these situations.

Love in my family was a word spoken, but not felt. When I married at 21, it was to the first woman to whom I felt a sexual attraction. This confusion about love and sex eventually destroyed my 13-year marriage, and deeply hurt the two sons I helped bring into this world. At this point is when my personal troubles began.

I eventually went through another four-year marriage, divorced, dated another woman for ten years, and then met and married still another woman for five years. The disaster from this last relationship was devastating financially, emotionally, and physically. I lost my home, was laid off from work, and my former partner filed criminal charges against me. I found myself at a new low. Stress from the ordeal took a physical toll requiring two years of medical doctor visits to correct.

Given my upbringing, I learned to tackle life's difficulties in my usual manner—under my own power and in my own way. I cried out to God and asked why? Meanwhile, I battled everything else in my headstrong, bullheaded way. I was met with further disappointment, which was followed by me at times screaming at God. Looking back at my actions now, I'm appalled by my behavior, but I didn't know any other way.

How did I get to this place in my life God?

We bring our upbringing, our family history, and any idiosyncrasies we've learned along the way into our life, and they influence how we deal with the challenges of living. Combine the social issues we face daily of high unemployment, mass killings, and drugs into the mix, and we now have a recipe for a cataclysmic event. In the chaotic mess of my life, I eventually boarded the proverbial bullet train of depression and hopelessness, racing toward my eventual doom.

When my last marriage ended in early 2010, I did return to church, in hopes of finding something but had no idea what. It felt good to be around other church people, and I somehow wanted God to save me from my chosen mess. Nothing changed, and nothing happened. I was a robot going through the motions and had no idea why or how to change it. Then I met my last relationship, a widow and someone whom I thought was ideal for me. My damaged pattern was once again repeated.

Like always before, I took charge of my life and made the decisions. Everything seemed right with this person, and I found someone with whom I was compatible. It all worked well for slightly over a year—until the bottom fell out again. Within days, my serene life inverted, and I was forced to move out. A terrific friend extended a helping hand and let me crash on her sofa. I then sank into another new low.

Evaluating my life was useless. It added up to zero. I had nothing to show for 61 years of hard work, no spouse, no family, no home, and no job. Empty and meaningless, life spiraled into a vortex of negative thoughts. These included suicide. I was desperate and trying to resolve inside my head why it would be okay to end it all. No one would care, and I doubt anyone would miss me. If you're thinking I was mired in self-loathing and pity, you're correct, but when you're in the middle of that mess, it doesn't look like self-pity. It just hurts.

Emotionally I felt raw, naked, and doomed to utter failure. I became a modern-day version of the biblical Job. Only one problem, unlike Job, I wasn't a righteous man that God was allowing the devil to test. I was a product of my own doing and choices. Self-reliance had failed me, and the results of my choices were glaringly awful.

I convinced myself that I was hopeless, and God could not and would never love me. Fortunately, I was mistaken. In the Bible, there are men just like me. For example, in the Old Testament there was a man named Balaam (pronounced bale-lem).[10] He was a headstrong person too. He also took charge of everything in his life and ruled with his emotions. He was riding his donkey one day (in the Bible they call it an ass). God was trying to get Balaam's attention and have him do something specific, but Balaam had his own ideas. Therefore, God ignored Balaam and worked with the donkey.

Balaam wanted the donkey to go a particular direction, but the ass disobeyed since the donkey was following God's orders. Frustrated, Balaam then beat the donkey with a rod; in fact, he did so three times. According to Numbers 22:28–30 (GNT) it reads:

> *"Then God gave the donkey the power of speech, and it said to Balaam, 'What have I done to you? Why have you beaten me these three times?' Balaam answered, 'Because you have made a fool of me! If I had a sword, I would kill you.' The donkey replied, 'Am I, not the same donkey on which you have ridden all your life? Have I ever treated you like this before?' 'No,' he answered."*

Like Balaam, God was trying to get my attention, but I wasn't listening. The direction of my path was the wrong way, and I wasn't willing to heed any other advice but my own. It was going to take some serious action to stop me in my tracks. When looking back at my current situation, I see it ended in utter disaster and ruin because God was trying to gain my attention. The big question: Would I listen?

Your story may be similar or not, but I'm sure you can identify with certain aspects of my story. The turmoil you're faced with may be different. Nonetheless, the same questions remain. Are you continually feeling depressed, losing hope, and feel there is no way out?

You see, it's not that your story is worse than mine, or someone else's. When you're losing hope, your situation is all that matters to you. Everyone around you seems happy, but you're hurting, silently screaming for help and at the same time, you know no one can help or understand what you're going through. You feel alone.

This is why it's so easy for us to internalize suicide—*I'm alone, no one can help, I might as well remove me from the picture*—an event everyone will miss. In my own life, I didn't try to act out my plan, but I thought long and hard on the idea of suicide. Those around me were unaware of my thoughts and pain. It was easy to fool everyone by hiding my pain, telling them lies about how I felt inside and mostly because they didn't ask.

When I first spoke the prayer at the end of my previous chapter, nothing happened. I didn't get all excited and run down the street hitting people in the face with my Bible. I felt a little better, but for the most part, I felt empty inside. That's normal.

Just because, you walk up to a stranger's house, knock on their door, and they invite you in, doesn't mean you'll feel safe or comfortable. In addition, the stranger isn't going to trust you openly. That takes time. You have to get to know the stranger. The only thing we've done so far is knock on heaven's door, and God extended His invitation.

All my life I identified myself as religious. I would pray, but not often. I attended church most of the time. I gave money some of the time. For me, going to church was a way to get to heaven, and I didn't commit much more than that. I tried living a "good" life and looked the part on Sundays, even though I wasn't so "good" during the week. If my guilt got the best of me, I'd confess my failures to God, feel better, and then continued as before. I did read the Bible through several times and felt I was doing okay, but I was still stuck in depression.

I have a friend whom I met in 1987 while living in Germany. We've remained in contact over the years on a random basis. Sometimes years slipped by before we'd reconnect, but when we did, we'd pick upright where we left off. I'm not sure how it began, but we recently started exchanging emails. In my messages, the feelings of desperation and hopelessness were interwoven in the emails. She then sent me a reply I'll never forget. It was a message of hope, of reassurance, and it was especially timely.

Feeling lost, desperate, and alone, I figured God had given up on me, and I was about to give up my life. She sent me words from the Bible that pierced through the darkness I was experiencing. I was about to discover that God wanted my attention and that my choices, until now, were not helping my situation. She sent me Jeremiah 29:11–13 (New King James – NKJ):

> *"For I know the thoughts I think toward you, says the Lord, thoughts of peace and not of evil, to give you a future and a hope. Then you will call on Me and go and pray to Me, and I will listen to you. And you will seek Me and find Me, when you search for Me with all your heart."*

Up to this point, I was feeling the whole world was against me, that life was useless and that God was punishing me for all my selfish choices. Clearly, I had something to learn, and it involved a promising future and tons of hope. What seemed like a new revelation, I discovered that God had a plan for me, which gave me hope that my life could be different. After receiving my friend's email, I prayed the same prayer we read at the end of the previous chapter. In fact, let's read it again.

God, I am asking You to hear these words. Send Angels to watch over and protect me. I feel depressed and hopeless, and can't make sense of life, but I want to know You. Help me to understand the words of the Bible and push all the negative thoughts out of my head.

As I said earlier, afterward nothing happened. Lightning didn't flash across the sky, I didn't win the lottery, people weren't suddenly kind to me, and my life wasn't perfect either. But, I did notice I felt better, and I wanted to know more, especially about God's feelings toward me.

My life started in a new direction. I began a new journey. This time I wanted to know the truth about God, not what other people were saying about God or the Bible, but the truth for me. I was thirsty for knowledge about God, and I opened my first metaphorical door.

My first step was a weak one. I had no foundation to work on, but at least I was taking a step in the right direction. I didn't see radical changes, and I was clinging to the edge of life, but determined to claw my way back to a better life.

These steps can work for you. So, are you willing to join me and listen to what God is trying to tell us? If so, then we have found an excellent starting point. If not, prepare to face further disappointments. It took me 61 years to wake up to my selfishness. I'm hoping you'll catch on much quicker. By the way, if you're older than me, and facing these issues, please accept my apology. It's not about the age; it's about getting our lives going in the right direction. Would you care to join me in this journey?

Reviewing this Chapter

Are you willing to take the first step and join me in this journey?

_____

_____

_____

_____

_____

_____

_____

How has your past influenced who you are today?

_____

_____

_____

_____

_____

_____

_____

Can you identify areas in your life where God is trying to gain your attention?

_____

_____

_____

_____

_____

_____

_____

_____

_____

Chapter 4

Hanging by a Thread

Earlier I talked about the selections we make in life. My life's choices were not helping me, and at 61, the results of my decisions added up to zilch. Don't get me wrong. I didn't deliberately make unwise choices. In fact, I gave my decisions great thought. I weighed the alternatives, how they influenced my life, future, and happiness. *So where had I gone wrong? At what point does my life get easier?*

I have an aunt who is 104 this year. She's smart, funny and knows the answers to most game show questions. Alert and aware, she can discuss current events. She has broken and replaced both hips; she has also dislocated one shoulder and broke the other in a fall. Blind in one eye because of cataracts, slightly deaf, she fell and broke her neck once and recovered, but she is always quick with a smile and something positive. Her attitude and spirit—not to mention living over one hundred years—make her my hero. With this person to influence me, you'd think I could get on with my mess and lead a happy life.

In the Old Testament (Second Samuel 11:1–27), there is a story about a young man named David. When he was teenager, he was a shepherd and managed a flock of sheep. He was remarkably accurate with a slingshot; in fact he once knocked a tall bad-guy unconscious with a smooth river rock. He became the local hero for that brave act. Eventually, he became king. David was good-looking, and he liked music and played an instrument. Life was good for David.

Just to give you a glimpse into David as an individual if we look in the New Testament at Acts 13:22 (NKJ), we see a clear picture of how God felt about David:

> *"He (God) raised up for them David as king, to whom also He (God) gave testimony and said, 'I have found David the son of Jesse, a man after My own heart, who will do all My will.'"*

It doesn't get any better than that, especially when God is saying these things about a person. However, like many of us, David also made selfish and unwise decisions. And, not just one bad decision, David made a series of bad choices that compounded his problems.[11]

For example, when David's army was out in battle one spring, he stayed home rather than lead his army. David had multiple wives and was up on the rooftop one early evening when he spotted a beautiful woman bathing in another house. It's distressing enough that David was home, instead of leading his army like most kings, but spying on a woman taking a bath wasn't wise either.

It didn't take long for King David to identify this woman as Bathsheba, but unfortunately, she was married. Bathsheba and David had an affair, and now the king wanted her for a wife. To complicate the situation, Bathsheba becomes pregnant from the affair.

The king sends for Bathsheba's husband Uriah and calls him in from the battle. After asking Uriah about the war, he encourages Uriah to go home and sleep with his wife Bathsheba. However, Uriah sleeps at the door to David's house. When David asks why, Uriah tells the king that as long as his fellow soldiers are away from their wives, sleeping on the ground, and faced with a war, he cannot with a clear conscience, sleep at home with his wife. This frustrates David.

Several attempts to get Uriah to sleep with his wife fail, making the situation tense for the king. Nevertheless, David will make more unwise decisions. David sends Uriah, to the front lines of the battle, carrying a specific message from the king, to the field commander. The commander is to place Uriah in the worst part of the battle, and then the commander is to withdraw the other soldiers, leaving Uriah alone.

It works, and Uriah dies. Indirectly, David has committed murder, and this is on top of adultery with another man's wife. Because David was king he got away with his actions socially, but God wasn't going to allow this to go unnoticed. A messenger, called a prophet, carried word to King David telling him that God knew what David had done.[12] God was trying to get David's attention.

It wasn't one poor judgment that got David into trouble. The natural progression of his decisions amassed into a huge pile of dung. As a result, fear, depression, hopelessness, desperation, and isolation are just some of the feelings David experienced solely because of his choices. Perhaps, the decisions of your life weren't this grave. In fact, in the midst of my troubles, I even said to God once; *"Hey, I'm nowhere near as evil as this guy, David. It doesn't seem fair that my life is this miserable. Can't You give me a break, God!"*

Whether my crimes were equal to or less than David's wasn't the issue. I chose to run my life my own selfish way, which made my actions no different from those of David. The mess in my life was a result of continuous selfish decisions that did not include God. In my mind, I was hanging by a thread, between death and the miserable existence I knew. But, who was ultimately responsible for my mess?

I had no one to blame but myself. It was my decisions that placed me in this space. When I chose to change the direction of my life and enter the door leading to my new journey, it was just the beginning. Moving in my new direction would require effort on my part to make the changes. I feared that old habits would get in the way, and at first, I wasn't sure if I could do it. Thank goodness, I'm not alone and not the first person to feel this way.

On the night before the New Testament Jesus died on a cross, he cried out to Heaven. Jesus asked God, if there could be another choice, other than dying. The urgency of Jesus's groaning was so intense that it caused the man to sweat drops of blood.[13] The medical term for it is Hematidrosis[14] and is a rare condition in which a human sweats blood. It may occur when a person is suffering extreme levels of stress—for example, facing his or her own death. The difference between Jesus's cry for help and my own is that Jesus said the ultimate choice was up to God.

My life's choices have always been about me, and I wanted God to put a stamp of approval on my decisions, not the other way around. By making my own decisions without input from God, by taking charge solely by myself, I was going about it all wrong. I never thought what I was doing was wrong. It's just that after all this time, and finding nothing but a mess, I needed a new path, a new way of doing things.

About this time in a troubled person's life, that person might turn to self-help books, seminars, mediation, hypnosis, drugs, and a host of things that may or may not help. Some of the things I've listed are good, and maybe of help, but they don't solve the base issue. It's like placing a Band-Aid over an open sore, without treating the wound first. Although the things listed above will treat the symptoms, they cannot resolve the underlying problems.

When Jesus was teaching, he had many men and women who followed him. There were twelve men Jesus handpicked to be his apostles. The word "apostle" is classical Greek meaning "one who is sent away." Today, we call these individuals ambassadors. These men, selected from a broad range of occupations and educations, were chosen to spread the message Jesus was teaching. Several fishermen, a tax collector, a doctor—we know some apostles only by their name. They were men that few leaders would ever select!

One of the men was named Peter, and he caught fish for a living. Rough, hardy, strong, Peter was a stocky man with a talent for pulling in loaded nets. It's backbreaking work to pull fishing nets into a boat manually. Peter was also headstrong, opinionated, short-tempered, feisty, and could be rash. Jesus considered Peter to be his friend and close ally.[15]

Before his arrest, Jesus told his friends that they would scatter and hide during this time.[16] Then in Luke 22:33 (NKJ) Peter in his bold manner stated; *"Lord, I am ready to go with You, to prison and to death."* Jesus told Peter that before the morning rooster crows; you will deny you even knew Me (Jesus) three times. That night after Jesus was arrested, Peter denied knowing Jesus three times, even using swearing language at one point to make his protest. As Jesus predicted, when Peter heard the rooster crow, guilt washed over the strong man, reducing him to tears.[17] Later in this story, though, Jesus forgives Peter and tells him he is of great value to God.

When we make decisions that are selfish, and choose to consider only ourselves, we'll inevitably fail. My decisions were no different from those of Peter, and I had failed. Therefore, the root-cause of depression is often our failures. If these failures persist without change, they will eventually lead to a loss of hope.

Personal failures may occur in relationships, jobs, starting a new business, our family of origin, and even our friends. For some people, it's easy to shrug off these kinds of failures, but if you're like me, they can add up over time. Mine were a series of failures over many years. When I finally was left with nothing, the pain was too extensive. At some point, I begin to question if the whole world was against me. Unfortunately, this experience is usually followed by feelings of anger.

Reviewing this Chapter

Do you feel you are making decisions for yourself but not receiving satisfaction from those choices?

_____

_____

_____

_____

_____

_____

Provide a recent example when you choose a particular path and it seemed like you failed to reach your objective.

_____

_____

_____

_____

_____

_____

Do you find yourself focusing on your failures, and experiencing anger?

_____

_____

_____

_____

_____

_____

_____

_____

If you knew God was praying for you and waiting for you to turn to Him for answers, how would that make you feel?

_____

_____

_____

_____

_____

_____

_____

_____

Chapter 5

Desperate and Angry

After I made the decision not to choose death by my own hands, then the anger set in. Not only was I desperate for change, but now I was angry about my past. It didn't stop there. I was angry at the world for being so cruel; angry toward my parents for doing a lousy job; and angry with God for not taking my life when He had so many opportunities. *Why had I been born?*

In many ways, divorce can feel like a death, only without having a body and the funeral. After my third divorce, the process of getting past the emotions and pain wasn't getting easier. The ending of each successive relationship cost me financially, emotionally, and physically. Despite good intentions of family and friends, getting through this ordeal, required time and healing. For a while, I would spend countless hours scolding myself with negative self-talk. I was the common denominator in my failed relationships, and I accepted nearly all the blame. My thoughts fueled the anger, and I had plenty of reasons to be angry.

Once I headed down the anger path, it was easy to shift my focus back onto thoughts of suicide. A constant battle raged inside my head with two separate voices arguing, which created confusion. This produced more anger and frustration. It was a vicious cycle, and I thought it would never end. Then one day, the friend who had given me her sofa to sleep on, shared some wisdom with me. It started with her rhetorical questions:

"Are you willing to make a change for your future that will be different from your past? What have you learned about your past that you don't want to repeat in the future?"

Her last question was the easiest to answer. What have I learned about my past that I don't want to repeat in my future? Tons; I never want to repeat my past! In reality, I wasn't focused on the first part of her question because I hadn't analyzed the lessons I've learned. I centered on the pain of my past and felt angry about it. Figuring out what I learned from my past mistakes was critical and I eventually began to write my thoughts out in a journal (forming the basis of this book).

Her first question about my willingness to make a change was insulting. Of course, I was willing. Only I wasn't changing anything that would affect my future. Clearly, this was going to be a personal challenge. After mulling these questions over, I expressed my frustration with trying to shake off my negative thoughts. She suggested that I should recite a particular prayer from the Bible whenever I found myself in such a negative emotional state.

Her suggestion is a familiar verse that you may know, called Psalm 23 (GNT):

"The Lord is my shepherd; I have everything I need. He lets me rest in fields of green grass and leads me to quiet pools of fresh water. He gives me new strength. He guides me in the right paths as he has promised. Even if, I go through the deepest darkness, I will not be afraid, Lord, for you are with me. Your shepherd's rod and staff protect me. You prepare a banquet for me, where all my enemies can see me; you welcome me as an honored guest and fill my cup to the brim. I know that your goodness and love will be with me all my life, and your house will be my home as long as I live."

At first, I found myself reciting this verse repeatedly. If you're like me, and struggling with anger and frustration, I suggest you try reading this prayer; it works at diminishing your internal anger. As before, read the words aloud so you can hear yourself. In no time, you'll notice that your anger is less frequent and you're not spending as much time focusing on your frustrations. This is just another figurative door leading to more truth, as mentioned in earlier chapters.

Now, I noticed something else: I had been scolding myself for making "bad" decisions. When one's choices are analyzed, the result is one of two products—either the outcome matches my expectation, or it does not. When I didn't get the outcome I wanted, I was angry. It reminded me of children who throw a temper tantrum when denied something. By being angry at the "wrong" outcome, I labeled my decision as "bad" and beat myself up about it. This attitude was juvenile and immature.

Psalm 37:8 (GNT) says this concerning my actions; *"Don't give in to worry or anger; it only leads to trouble."*

Then in Proverbs 14:29(GNT) it says; *"If you stay calm, you are wise, but if you have a hot temper, you only show how stupid you are."*

Finally, in James 1:19(GNT) it says; *"Remember this, my dear friends! Everyone must be quick to listen, but slow to speak and slow to become angry."*

By being angry with God, the world, my parents, or even life, I was focusing my attention on the wrong source. In truth, I was angry with myself but didn't want to admit it. In reciting Psalm 23, I slowly shook off the negative feelings, and I found the anger slowly fading. This doesn't happen overnight. For some, it may take a long time to process through the anger.

As I stated earlier in this book, if you're lucky enough to afford counseling, or have a priest, pastor, or rabbi to confide in, I urge you to exercise those options. Don't wait. Make the call. Since anger is about perception, we can't stay focused on the negative, because this will only lead us to see what's wrong with our situation.

My anger was directed internally and about my bad decisions. I wrestled with why I was angry and the sources of my anger and in each case, it boiled down to my selfish decisions and me. If I believed Psalm 23 and the Lord is my shepherd, then I must have everything I need. I started making this my personal goal—to live life as if all my needs were met. Anytime I felt I had needs, then I would shift my attitude and live in expectation the Lord is meeting my needs, but I hadn't seen it yet.

Remember earlier, I also quoted Jeremiah 29:11–13 (NKJ):

"For I know the thoughts I think toward you, says the Lord, thoughts of peace and not of evil, to give you a future and a hope. Then you will call on Me and go and pray to Me, and I will listen to you. And you will seek Me and find Me, when you search for Me with all your heart."

So you see, suffering isn't part of God's plan; it's our own decisions that place us there. By making the small changes I've listed so far, I began to shift my view about my life. This is why I have been asking you to read aloud particular words in this book. Change in our life will only occur when we disrupt old patterns and stop obsessing about the bad.

I've asked you to read several prayers along our journey to discover the truth about God and life. Now I think we're ready for the next prayer. As before, read this aloud and often as you feel it necessary:

God, thank You for hearing the words I'm reading. Thank You for sending Angels to watch over and protect me. I feel angry and frustrated, and honestly don't like my life up to this point, but I want to know the truth about You. Help me to understand the words of the Bible and focus on how much You care about me.

In the following step of our journey, I will reveal how much God cares about you. In addition, I explain what He's doing to show His love for you and me.

Reviewing this Chapter

Do you feel your anger is leading to further depression?

_____

_____

_____

_____

_____

_____

Would you try reciting Psalm 23 to see if it will help you shake-off the negative feelings?

_____

_____

_____

_____

_____

_____

_____

Do you scold yourself for bad decisions?

_____

_____

_____

_____

_____

_____

_____

_____

Can you accept the concept that God doesn't want you to suffer?

_____

_____

_____

_____

_____

_____

_____

_____

If you had a choice, would you want or desire a future and hope?

_____

_____

_____

_____

_____

_____

_____

_____

If you could picture your ideal future, what would it look like?

_____

_____

_____

_____

_____

_____

_____

_____

Chapter 6

Coupons

When I was young, my mother would go shopping and return home with *S&H* or *Blue-Chip* trading stamps.[18] Retailers gave them away with each purchase. Booklets could be obtained, and my siblings and I would sit around the dining table licking the back of the stamps and pasting them into the booklets. Converting the individual and coils of stamps into booklets was time-consuming.

There were redemption stores for both stamp varieties. Carting armloads of these filled booklets to the redemption center; mother could exchange the booklets for household items, like toasters, ironing boards, dishes, blenders, and many other items. For us children, it was like receiving something free, and it was exciting. Often our family could get things we couldn't typically afford.

Trading stamps faded over time and they were replaced by the manufacturer's coupons. The coupons work the same way, because the buyer receives something free or at a reduced price by redeeming the coupon at the store. In fact, collecting coupons has now blossomed into a thriving business, with some individuals creating groups to exchange or trade them.[19]

Whether a coupon, or trading stamps, or even if a gift card is used, when you redeem something, it is an exchange for a benefit. Redemption means to exchange. Therefore, to move forward in my personal journey, I needed to exchange my past for a benefit. I needed to redeem my failures.

By choosing to be my own boss, I became self-reliant. This individuality isn't wrong, and society teaches us to walk this path as a way to achieve independence and sometimes success. But, when things didn't have the outcome I expected, and this repeated pattern happened many times, I became discouraged, depressed, and lost hope.

Now up to this point, my life's choices hadn't been kind to me. Desperate, I needed to exchange my failures for something that would lead me away from self-destruction. When I started on my journey, I discovered that I couldn't survive on my poor choices and following the same patterns of decision-making. I needed help.

The next step in my journey revealed that anger was not helping my situation. As long as I held onto the anger, my life was stuck in negative thoughts, again leading to self-destruction. Then I discovered that being a control-freak was my source of failure. My developed attitude that "I know how to fix things" was my enemy. When I failed to achieve the outcome I expected, I could only blame myself, thereby perpetuating the feelings of self-loathing. I needed a way out of this mess and what I'm about to share worked for me. I believe it can work for you too, if you're willing to try it.

To discover the truth about God and the Bible, the following step in your journey will be life changing. Like the trading stamps that my mother exchanged for a benefit, the information I'm about to share with you will be a benefit beyond what you may think you already know. We're going to discover how we can exchange or redeem our failures, depression, hopelessness, bad decisions, wrong outcomes, and anger for something fantastic. I've touched on the subject briefly when I shared the story about the two criminals dying on the cross next to Jesus.

Remember to keep an open mind. I am aware that simply quoting some phrases out of the Bible does not make me an expert in theology. I recommend you read the Bible for yourself and verify what I'm sharing. Don't just take my word for it either or anyone else for that matter. You must seek this information for yourself.

Redemption is a key ingredient to discovering the truth.[20] We must exchange that part of us that has failed, for something better—more helpful. Although the concepts of this exchange have been occurring for years, it may be a new idea for you. Our failures, selfishness, and attitudes can result in death. It's not a physical death, although sometimes it can cause this—I'm talking about the death of one's soul.

In 1901, a doctor named Dr. Duncan MacDougall placed dying patients on a scale to find the weight of a human soul.[21] The soul is believed to leave one's body at the time of death. Dr. MacDougall found that humans weighed 21 grams less, after they died. Therefore, he concluded the weight of the human soul is 21 grams. His findings published in the *Journal of The American Society for Physical Research* in March 1907.

He fixed a measurable weight for the human soul, but he found no similar measurements with animals that died. This clearly identifies a part of humans not found in any other creature on earth and this spirit disappears upon a human's death. So, if the soul or human spirit leaves the body when we die, where does it go?

Let's return to the story of Jesus's crucifixion and the two criminals hanging on crosses on either side of Jesus. One of the criminals who sought God, confessed his crimes, and found hope.[22] The hope and meaning for the criminal's life were always available. It's just the criminal made other choices and selected his own path. When he realized this mistake, God gave the man purpose to his life and told him he would go to heaven and be with Jesus. In essence, the criminal exchanged his failures, anger, and hopelessness, where God redeemed his confession for a benefit—going to heaven to be with Jesus. His impending physical death is replaced with hope for his soul.

In the New Testament of the Bible (Romans 3:23 GNT) it reads; *"Everyone has sinned and is faraway from God's saving presence."* We can't avoid this sin because our human nature keeps us from being what God expects. By the way, the definition of *sin* is a failing, crime, wrongdoing, indulgence, and misbehavior—even selfishness. Our sin, or human nature, comes with a cost. In Romans 6:23 (New Living Translation – NLT) it says this; *"For the wages (or payment) of sin is death, but the gift of God is eternal life through Christ Jesus our Lord."* The criminal who died next to Jesus, received the exchange of his sin, for going to heaven to be with Jesus. His soul saved from, and redeemed for, life in heaven.

How is this possible you ask? The apostles who were listening to Jesus speak, once asked this same question. In Matthew 19:25–26 (GNT) it reads:

> *"The disciples were astounded. 'Then who in the world can be saved?' They asked. Jesus looked at them intently and said, 'Humanly speaking, it is impossible. But with God everything is possible.'"*

The steps to achieve this redemption can be found in Romans 10:9–10 (GNT), for it further states:

> *"If you confess that Jesus is Lord and believe that God raised him from death, you will be saved. For it is by our faith that we are put right with God; it is by our confession that we are saved."*

In essence, the criminal performed this same exercise with Jesus, on the day he was dying.

So, how and why does God make this exchange or redemption possible?

Earlier I stated that no one honestly knows exactly 100% what happens when we die, or what's on the other side. If the Bible is interpreted from a literal perspective, then it states exactly what happens if we <u>don't</u> accept the redemption process shared in the previous paragraphs. It is nothingness, empty, void, and you're not in heaven. This is not what I want to happen for my belief system.

In Hebrews 11:1 (GNT) it says that our belief system in God involves faith and hope; *"To have faith is to be sure of the things we hope for, to be certain of the things we cannot see."* Since some people may wonder, what's on the other side of death, they must choose to accept there is nothing, or what was shared earlier—heaven. Without redemption, faith, and hope, our innate human nature leaves us out of heaven and separate from God, but that's not God's plan.

As stated earlier in Jeremiah 29:11 (NKJ), God shares His plan for us:

> *"I alone know the plans I have for you, plans to bring you prosperity and not disaster, plans to bring about the future you hope for."*

For some of us, to take the next step in our journey, we must be bold, and have faith to enter the unknown. There may be some of you, who have taken this step at an earlier time in your life, but you now find yourself discouraged and losing hope. If you're like me, this isn't the first time you've taken this brave step. For me, my personal failings kept me from progressing past a certain point. I was stuck in the asking for forgiveness from God, but repeating the same patterns of my past. After a while, I felt I was beyond redemption, and that God had given up all hope in seeing me move forward in my journey. However, I was wrong.

Earlier I talked about a man named Peter, who was a friend of Jesus. When Jesus was arrested, right before his crucifixion, this apostle Peter denied Jesus's existence when questioned by the government.[23] Despite taking earlier bold steps of redemption—the ones I've been discussing—Peter's personal failures kept him from progressing forward. When our failures to meet God's expectations are foremost on one's mind, it's difficult to have hope or faith. Although there's more to this story, than just admitting our failures. There is forgiveness, and grace.

In the New Testament, Jesus had kind words for Peter's upcoming denial. In Luke 22:31–32 (GNT) Jesus talks with His friend (He calls Peter by his given name, Simon):

> *"Simon, Simon! Listen! Satan has received permission to test all of you, to separate the good from the bad as a farmer separates the wheat from the chaff. But I have prayed for you, Simon, that your faith will not fail. And when you turn back to Me, you must strengthen your brothers."*

Jesus knew the future and saw that Peter was going to fail. He told Peter that when he returned to the step of exchange and redemption afterward, Peter would be an inspiration to others. This action is called grace, which means unmerited favor. Peter could not earn this favor from God, he needed to ask for forgiveness and return to the journey. Peter had stopped his journey because of failures, but God wanted more for Peter.

According to Romans 8:34 (GNT):

> *"Who, then, will condemn them? (The sinners of this world) Not Christ Jesus, who died, or rather, who was raised to life and*

*is at the right side of God, pleading (communicating) with Him
(God) for us!"*

Also in John 17:20 (NKJ), Jesus speaks the following prayer:

*"I do not pray for these alone, but also for those who will believe in
Me through their (the followers of Jesus) word; that they all may be
one, as You, Father, are in Me, and I in You; that they also may be
one in Us, the world may believe that You sent Me."*

Prayer or intercession is the same as communicating. Jesus is in direct
communication with God about you and me. This means when you and
I fail, Jesus is praying for us—not just praying for us either, but also
needing us to return to our journey of discovering the truth about God.
This is called hope, and it requires our faith. One cannot fail and be lost,
for there is always hope with Jesus. I don't know about you, but when
I read that Jesus is praying for me before I fail, and He is hoping for
me to return, this is a humbling experience. God loves us this much.

To stress this aspect of God's love, words written in the Old Testament
make a strong case. In Numbers 23:19 (NLT) it reads:

*"God is not a man that He should lie. He is not a human that He
should change his mind. Has He ever spoken and failed to act? Has
He ever promised and not carried it through?"*

The message is straightforward, God doesn't fail us; we fail ourselves.
God doesn't give up on us, nor does He change his mind about us.
The interesting thing about the above Old Testament scripture is
Baleem—the person mentioned earlier, who wasn't doing what God
wanted him to do out of stubbornness and beat his ass three times in
anger—spoke this message!

We could choose our own path, make our own decision, and run
the risk of denying the existence of God, but where will it get us? Or,
we could be like the criminal who recognized his mistakes, confessed
those errors, and asked for God's help. It took me a long time to awaken
to my errors and do something about it. I was deceiving myself into

thinking *I'll just convince God to bless my plans and only call on Him when things get tough*. My realization that this plan was a failure, forced me to seek out the truth about God and His plans for me. This decision required changes in my thoughts and actions, but more importantly, my new path provided me with the truth about my past situation and the mistakes I was making. This time around, I've held nothing back and have given God 100% of me—mind, body and heart. This wasn't an easy decision either.

It's like standing on the beach and seeing the waves rolling onto shore. The water looks cold and scary, yet someone in the water is saying it's not that frightening. In a bold act of faith, you must trust what the person is telling you and experience it for yourself.

Walking through the door of truth about what God wants of us, demands this same act of faith and boldness. It is life changing and yes, it will seem scary at first. I can assure you though, that God is waiting to hear from you. When you're ready to press on with your journey, then read the next prayer—a prayer of redemption. Again, read this aloud:

> *God, thank You for hearing the words I'm reading. Thank You for sending Angels to watch over and protect me. Thank You for praying for me, even though I didn't know it. I'm getting to know who You are, and I'm ready to enter the door of truth. I want to know more. Forgive me for my selfishness, my failures, and for not including You in my life. Help me to understand faith and hope. Open new doors of truth for me so I may know even more about You.*

You've just made the greatest decision of your life. There's more work ahead, but we will through this book journey together or, we can directly walk together. If you've completed the above prayer, and wish to share this with me, I'd be delighted to hear from you. At the end of this book is my contact information, please email me and tell me about your decision. I want to celebrate with you. You've joined what I call God-seekers.

Now that you've made the decision to be a God-seeker, there are more things to learn that will enable you to understand God's plan for us and our individual purpose. In the following chapters of this book, we'll discover what is expected of us as God-seekers, and the source of many of life's disappointments—our enemy, Satan. This is the part of our journey where we prepare for the future.

I said in the beginning of this book, we've only knocked on someone's door. You've just been invited into Jesus's house, and now He wants to show you around, get you familiar with each room, have dinner with you, and have you meet the other guests there with you.

Reviewing this Chapter

Have you ever felt you were beyond help or that God didn't care about you?

_____

_____

_____

_____

_____

_____

You just exchanged and redeemed your failures for a hope in the future. What does that mean to you?

_____

_____

_____

_____

_____

_____

In your own words, describe how you feel now about your life and your future.

_____

_____

_____

_____

_____

_____

_____

_____

Intermission

Time To Take A Breather

Everything I've shared up to point has lead us to the redemption of our failures in exchange for hope. This journey has been a systematic process building one idea on another.

You've made the choice to become a God-seeker. However, if we stopped our journey here, declaring we arrived, it would be no better than sending you to the North Pole on an expedition, but outfitted with equipment for a beach trip to Hawaii. This would be a huge mistake. Nonetheless, many well-intentioned individuals who lead God-seekers to the point we reached in this past chapter, have made this same mistake.

Our journey together to find our purpose and hope beyond the depression needs further steps along our path.[24] I want to equip you with the tools to move past the redemption prayer, and remain in a state of hope, journeying beyond where in my past I often remained stuck. Several times in my life, I reached the point of redemption, but failed to understand how to move forward. This was a barrier and a source of my depression. Along my journey, I've also met other individuals, who like me struggled to get past the redemption stage, letting me know I'm not alone in this struggle.

Earlier, I spoke about the twelve handpicked men Jesus selected to be his apostles.[25] These were not great leaders or famous men. They were individuals who failed to meet God's expectation; like Peter when he denied he knew Jesus, even though he and Jesus were friends. After witnessing Jesus's death, some of these men didn't believe the other apostles when they explained that they saw Jesus alive again. They had to see it for themselves. Thomas was one such apostle and when Jesus specifically asked Thomas to place his fingers in the crucifixion holes of Jesus's body, Thomas finally believed.[26]

These friends of Jesus, who had witnessed this man healing people, raising individuals from the dead, and who conquered death himself, scattered and hid themselves the day of Jesus's arrest and crucifixion. They weren't prominent leaders and often lacked formal educations, but this didn't stop Jesus from selecting these men.

To equip his friends for their futures, Jesus taught them wisdom, scriptures, parables, prayers, and placed his blessing on them. He sent them throughout their world to proclaim the Good News about Jesus.[27] We will need the same blessing and equipment for our journey.

In the Prologue of this book, I made a statement about my personal search for the truth. I said my path was; *"A journey that started long ago, interrupted, began again, sidetracked, and finally it showed me a glimpse of the truth I had missed along the way."* The reason for the interruption, and why I began again was just explained in the above paragraphs. I lacked the equipment and preparation for the journey beyond redemption. I was missing knowledge and wisdom.

When I finally discovered I lacked these two ingredients, it was my *"ah-ha"* moment. The missing parts of "knowledge and wisdom," and how these two can affect our journey, limited my hope. I was missing important tools. If one builds a house, that person will need the correct tools and information to carry out their objective—otherwise it will be a disaster. The house builder will have faith of a successful job and the hope of future value, when that builder possesses the right equipment and knowledge. Our God-seeker journey is no different.

Since our personal failures lead to anger and sometimes depression, it is important for us to be properly equipped and trained with the knowledge of our hope and future. We will need the correct tools. The journey is not easy and it will demand effort. Finally, I learned I could cast off the anchors of depression and move forward. No longer will I remain stuck with wanting death.

In the next few chapters, we will discover the necessary tools to carry out true growth and leave our past and depression behind us. We'll start by discovering true justice about those who've hurt us, and God's plan for the entire world. We'll learn why being around other God-seekers can help us on our journey, and why this path we've chosen isn't populated with millions of like-minded individuals. We'll discover who our enemy is and why he makes our life miserable, but most of all, we'll find out why we're on this journey. We will discover prospects that were planned long before our birth.[28]

Are you ready to join me and step forward?

Reviewing Everything So Far

What are the three most important elements you've learned up to this point in the book?

_____

_____

_____

_____

_____

_____

Are there any specific areas of the book that have given you encouragement or been helpful in your journey?

_____

_____

_____

_____

_____

_____

_____

Chapter 7

Justice

The anger I experienced about my personal and monetary losses only perpetuated my depression. I wanted to get even and punish those who caused me harm or at a minimum, have God send a bolt of lightning down and destroy them. But, I couldn't find anything in the Bible to support my desires. Sometimes, it's easier to blame God, rather than to accept the idea of our personal choices.

How many times have we heard or even said these words: *How can a just God allow children to die?* If not children, then substitute the word for a mother or father dying of cancer, or a friend, or sister, or brother. When we read about mass shootings in malls, theaters, schools, or public places, we want satisfaction, justice, and some of us will blame God.

The reality is this, the person pulling the trigger is responsible, and often, there are extenuating circumstances behind the gunman. Nonetheless, it was still the choice of the criminal and as a result, many innocent people suffer. Crimes make us angry and we want justice, so we pursue who we think is responsible with vengeance. Nonetheless, some of us will blame God for everything wrong.

Our current court system is overwhelmed with millions of cases dealing with crimes, lawsuits, and challenges to our Constitution. It's not a perfect system, for juries can make decisions based on their passions and sometimes let the guilty go free, or worse, they unjustly punish those who are innocent.

If the case concerns heinous crimes—ones that make us cringe when we hear the details—we then demand justice. When dealing with criminals, some folks may quote the Old Testament, where in Exodus 21:23–25 (NKJ) it reads:

"But if any harm follows, then you shall give life for life, eye for eye, tooth for tooth, hand for hand, foot for foot, burn for burn, wound for wound, stripe for stripe."

And according to Leviticus 24:17–18 (GNT):

"Any who commit murder shall be put to death, and any who kill an animal belonging to someone else must replace it."

When capital punishment was temporarily banished in the United States, juries sought life without parole for convicted individuals.[29] People figured once the criminal was locked away, the issue could be forgotten. Over time, capital punishment returned to some states and the process for executing convicted felons became long and arduous. For the families and friends of the victim or victims, their sense of justice is often not satisfied, which helps fuel the feelings of anger and depression.

Sometimes in court, defendants or witnesses lie, lawyers will cleverly twist the details, juries are blind, mistakes are made and someone who is innocent is unfairly convicted of a crime. Because we are human, we make mistakes. Thankfully, the long process to capital punishment allows new evidence to come forward, like DNA testing, and the once convicted are set free. Does this satisfy those who want justice?

In the New Testament, there was a woman who slept with a married man who was not her husband.[30] By Hebrew law, the adulterous woman was to be stoned to death, so the men of the community dragged her to the temple-church, seeking justice. Jesus was sitting on the steps, and the religious leaders quoted Old Testament Hebrew law concerning her crime. The leaders didn't like Jesus because He made claims about Himself that were baffling and seemed inconsistent with their laws.

Jesus could either agree with their Hebrew law, or He would incriminate Himself and the leaders would feel justified in attacking Jesus. When they quoted the law, they sought Jesus's answer, but He pretended He didn't hear them and began drawing in the sand with His finger. The leaders pushed Jesus for an answer, so He stood and faced the leaders. In John 8:7–9 (GNT) we read the following:

> *"As they stood there asking Him questions, He straightened up and said to them, 'Whichever one of you has committed no sin may throw the first stone at her.' Then He bent again and wrote on the ground. When they heard this, they all left, one by one, the older ones first. Jesus was left alone, with the woman still standing there."*

The story doesn't end here, and Jesus finishes the lesson by addressing the woman directly. John 8:10–11 (GNT) tells us what Jesus expected of the woman:

> *"He (Jesus) straightened up and said to her, 'Where are they? Is there no one left to condemn you?' 'No one, sir,' she answered. 'Well, then,' Jesus said, 'I do not condemn you either. Go, but do not sin again.'"*

This is how God's justice works. Even when you're caught breaking the law, God wants your agreement that you acted wrongly, expects you to confess your errors, and then He asks that you don't repeat the same mistake.

Like the criminal who died on the cross next to Jesus, the man wasn't spared from his punishment. The criminal agreed that he had committed criminal acts, and he asked Jesus for forgiveness. This action saved the criminal's soul, and he was granted entrance into heaven. God didn't punish the man, but the criminal's confession of sin saved him. Thankfully, God's justice isn't the same as those of men.

If you're asking, where is the justice for the woman caught in adultery? Consider the following information. In Luke 6:41, (NKJ) the Bible gives us instruction about judging another person:

"And why do you look at the speck in your brother's eye, but do not notice the plank in your own eye?"

The words in John as well as those in Luke are similar instructions—don't judge another person and don't seek justice unless you're without sin. In the New Testament, Romans 12:19–21 (GNT), we're given instructions on what is expected of us:

"Never take revenge, my friends, but instead let God's anger do it. For the scripture (Old Testament) says, 'I will take revenge, I will pay back, says the Lord.' Instead, as the scripture says: 'If your enemies are hungry, feed them; if they are thirsty, give them a drink; for by doing this you will make them burn with shame.' Do not let evil defeat you; instead, conquer evil with good."

Please note, I didn't say that if you're a victim of a crime, you shouldn't report it. Quite the contrary, the laws that govern society should be applied whenever necessary. However, when it comes to justice, let the courts and God take care of dispensing fairness. Never place justice in your own hands because we are all human and are subject to mistakes.

By now, you've probably noticed that I use the word God and Jesus as if they are the same person. They are, and they aren't. One of the things that upset the Hebrew leaders were the claims Jesus made about Himself. Jesus claimed equality with God in nature, power, and authority. These were bold statements. In John 5, Jesus healed a man on the Sabbath, which was a day of rest for Hebrews. Never mind that Jesus provided physical healing for a man who had been disabled for 38 years. The leaders were upset that Jesus was working on the day set aside for being in church.

In John 5:16–18 (GNT) this paragraph explains the attitude of the leaders:

"So they began to persecute Jesus, because he had done this healing on a Sabbath. Jesus answered them, 'My Father (referring to God) is always working, and I too must work.' This saying made the Jewish authorities all the more determined to kill him; not only had

*he broken the Sabbath law, but he had said that God was his own
Father and in this way had made himself equal to God."*

John 10:30 was even clearer about this claim when Jesus said; *"The
Father and I are one."*

Many words, from the Old to New Testaments, identify Jesus as
being the same as God, in power and authority. In addition, many
of them explain that Jesus was sent from God, whom Jesus called His
Father. Entire volumes of books try to explain this aspect of Jesus, and
it would take several chapters in my book to pursue it further. However,
I wanted to reveal the identity of Jesus and His relationship to God.

Earlier I quoted Romans 6:23 (NLT):

*"For the wages (or payment) of sin is death, but the gift of God
is eternal life through Christ Jesus our Lord."*

Because we are human, make mistakes, and are selfish, God is
justified in ignoring us. Nonetheless, because Jesus died, His death
justified us before God, so God can communicate with us. The Bible
isn't the only written source about Jesus. A man named Josephus, who
lived during the same time, wrote about events during the time of Jesus.
Josephus was like a reporter, who recorded the current events during
his life.[31] His writings have been translated into several languages, and
his book is readily available.

When Jesus died on the cross, He took on the responsibility of every
sin a man could ever commit. To explain this, John 3:16 (GNT) says this:

*"For God loved the world so much that He gave His only Son (Jesus),
so everyone who believes in Him may not die but have eternal life."*

Imagine standing before a judge who is about to sentence you to death.
But before it's proclaimed, Jesus steps to the bench and says, "Judge,
it's covered, I took this person's place and died for them." Through the
death of Jesus, we are justified to God and are forgiven. We are given the
right to go to heaven because of Jesus. How many people do you know
who would die for you?

In the previous chapter, you may have read aloud the prayer of redemption:

> *God, thank You for hearing the words I'm reading. Thank You for sending Angels to watch over and protect me. Thank You for praying for me, even though I didn't know it. I'm getting to know who You are, and I'm ready to enter the door of truth. I want to know more. Forgive me for my selfishness, my failures, and for not including You in my life. Help me to understand faith and hope. Open new doors of truth for me so I may know even more about You.*

Perhaps now, you understand why you're thanking God in this prayer. Long before you were born, Jesus died for you. In addition, Jesus has been praying for you because He wants to be friends with you.

Jesus didn't just die for you and me; He is alive and in heaven. After Jesus died on the cross, His followers buried him in a cave tomb. Then three days later, Jesus came back to life and walked out of the tomb. Jesus met many people on several occasions, even appearing before a crowd of 500 individuals. Jesus ate food and drank liquids to show the people He was alive and not a ghost. The total number of witnesses is never written, but during the 40 days Jesus appeared to many people, several references in the New Testament record the eyewitness accounts.[32]

The dead and now living Jesus is the principle foundation for God-seekers. Through His death and resurrection, Jesus covers our flaws and creates a path for us to communicate directly with God. We could complicate this message by adding scores of rules, dos and don'ts. In fact, some religions have done exactly that. The truth is, the message is simple, but it does require faith or a belief that what I've written is true. The only way you'll know for sure is to verify this for yourself— by reading the Bible.

If you've never read the Bible, I suggest you start now because it's never too late to start reading it. In fact, a great starting point is in the book of John, where I quoted from several times in this chapter of my book. The words of John provide understanding about God and Jesus, but they also reveal the love God has for us humans. In addi-tion, if you're like me and claimed to be a religious person, but weren't walking the talk, but now you're on the path to the truth, then John is an excellent place to start reading.

At this point, I hope you're still on this journey with me because there is more to learn. When you're ready, I have a new prayer for us to read aloud. This prayer incorporates everything we've learned so far:

> *God, thank You for hearing the words I'm reading. Thank You for sending Angels to watch over and protect me. Thank You for dying for me and praying for me, even though I didn't know it. I'm glad You are in my life because You have forgiven me for my selfishness and failures. I'm ready to continue forward and have You open new doors of truth for me. Give me wisdom so I can understand what I read in the Bible.*

Reviewing this Chapter

Has there been a time when you felt justice wasn't fair?

_____

_____

_____

_____

_____

_____

Do you blame God or did you take justice into our own hands?

_____

_____

_____

_____

_____

_____

_____

_____

Are you feeling like God is punishing or condemning you?

_____

_____

_____

_____

_____

_____

_____

_____

If you wanted God's forgiveness and it meant you must first forgive people who've hurt you, how would that affect you?

_____

_____

_____

_____

_____

_____

_____

_____

Chapter 8

This Can't Be True!

As a God-seeker we face challenges that will try to send us back to the place of depression. It's similar to driving a car. If we're not careful drivers, we can end up in a wreck. It isn't enough to prevent a crash just because we obey all the rules of driving. That is why we're taught defensive driving techniques—being watchful, looking down the road for possible trouble, and staying alert.

In the same way, we must be defensive God-seekers watching ahead for trouble, being aware, and alert to dangers that will risk our God-seeking journey. Earlier I mentioned that our root cause of depression could be our failures in life. When we said the redemption prayer, we exchanged our failures for forgiveness and Jesus wiped the slate clean. Unfortunately, errant individuals will cross our path and the dangers of crashing do not suddenly disappear. If we careen down our new journey's path without being defensive, we could easily find ourselves depressed again, and wondering how it happened.

Part of the defensive training to prevent accidents that cause further failures, is to learn about what to look out for, and being alert to the obstacles that cause God-seekers to stumble. In this chapter, we'll discuss the obstacles to our journey and learn how to overcome them.

Some of the greatest lessons in our defensive training come from the words spoken by Jesus. If you read the New Testament, you'll find that whenever Jesus spoke, he often used stories about people to teach a lesson. They're called parables. Now there is no sense in reinventing the wheel, and I couldn't have done a better job of explaining a parable, so I'll let the Wikipedia.org help explain what they are:[33]

> *"A parable is a succinct story, in prose or verse, which shows one or more instructive principles, or lessons, or (sometimes) a normative principle. It differs from a fable in that fables use animals, plants, inanimate objects, and forces of nature as characters, while parables feature human characters. It is a type of analogy."*

To help the people around him understand the hidden truths Jesus wanted to teach, he used parables. Jesus spoke about living a life that is good, about praying, about how to treat other people (even your enemies), about what is expected from God-seekers, the importance of learning wisdom, and many other topics. These parable were relevant to the society of that day so most common people could understand their meaning. In the first four chapters of the New Testament (the gospels of Matthew, Mark, Luke, and John), you'll find plenty of stories spoken by Jesus in the form of parables. The teachings by Jesus help God-seekers stay on track.

Jesus also said he would come back for all the God-seekers. When Jesus was about 30 years old,[34] he began teaching people, and his teaching period lasted only three and a half years.[35] In this short time, Jesus did a lot. After he died and came back to life three days later, he appeared to a multitude of people over a 40-day period. Then while people were speaking with him, Jesus disappeared to heaven.[36] Before leaving, he left instructions about His eventual return. The timing and date of his return are the source of many fervent religious speculations. The waiting period for His return can become an obstacle because we can become complacent, ignoring the need to stay vigilant in our journey.

In Matthew 24:42–44 (GNT), we read what Jesus says about the date of his return:

> *"Watch out, then, because you do not know what day your Lord will come. If the owner of a house knew the time when the thief would come, you can be sure that he would stay awake and not let the thief*

break into his house. So then, you also must always be ready, because the Son of Man (Jesus) will come at an hour when you are not expecting him."

This means, if anyone including a Rabbi, Priest, Pastor, Bible teacher, or the random individual who verbally attacks you while walking down the street, proclaims to know the actual day of Jesus' return, they're not speaking the truth.

What Jesus did say about the timing of his return is that we would see signs in the sky, activity in the earth's environment, and see world events that would lead to estimating how close we were to his return. In Luke 21:11 (NLT) Jesus says:

"There will be great earthquakes, and there will be famines and epidemics in many lands, and there will be terrifying things and great miraculous signs in the heavens."

Upon reading this information, my immediate thoughts center on the earthquake and tsunami in Japan, the outbreak of AIDS and Ebola in Africa, and the meteor that landed in Russia. In addition to this information, the Old Testament in the chapters of Daniel and Ezekiel give predictions about this period as well. Biblical scholars commonly refer to it as the "End Times" and another area of wide speculation.

In the New Testament, Paul writes to his friend in Second Timothy 3:1–5 (NLT) and talks about what life will be like during the end times:

"You should also know this, Timothy, that in the last days there will be difficult times. For people will love only themselves and their money. They will be boastful and proud, scoffing at God, disobedient to their parents, and ungrateful. They will consider nothing sacred. They will be unloving and unforgiving; they will slander others and have no self-control; they will be cruel and have no interest in what is good. They will betray their friends, be reckless, be puffed up with pride, and love pleasure rather than God. They will act as if they are religious, but they will reject the power that could make them godly. You must stay away from people like that."

Does this sound familiar to what's happening in our current society? Better yet, why is knowledge of these events even important? The better prepared we are as God-seekers, the lower the risk of crashing into obstacles that will cause us to fail on our journey. We must be prepared and now we will discover why this is important for us as God-seekers.

In this chapter of my book, I'm going to reveal two statements that may cause you to say, *"What? This can't be true!"*

Here is the first statement. When Jesus returns, he will take all the God-seekers who have said the redemption prayer you read earlier, and have spent their time continuously seeking God. The rest will be destroyed.[37] If we read Second Peter 3:10 (GNT), we'll see exactly what God says about this destruction:

> *"But the Day of the Lord will come like a thief. On that Day the heavens will disappear with a shrill noise, the heavenly bodies will burn up and be destroyed, and the earth with everything in it will vanish."*

Most people recognize that we have good and evil in the world. Most will agree there are unseen forces of good and bad. The good forces are from God, the evil forces are from the devil, also called Satan. Originally, Satan was an angel living in heaven. In a book called Enoch and in Genesis of the Bible, it describes what happened to Satan. He rebelled against God and felt he was the equivalent of God in power, and authority. Because of his rebellion, Satan was thrown out of heaven with one third of the angels who followed Satan. Their new home was on earth.[38] Satan is a God-seekers biggest obstacle. In the New Testament, Ephesians 6:12 (NLT), it tells us about Satan and his followers:

> *"For we are not fighting against people made of flesh and blood, but against the evil rulers and authorities of the unseen world, against those mighty powers of darkness who rule this world, and against wicked spirits in the heavenly realms."*

Scores of books, movies, and TV programs have depicted people owned and controlled by Satan. Most illustrations are meant to frighten us, but I assure you, the force of Satan is real. Themes from many movies portray the powers of evil battling the energies of good. A perfect example of this, are the *Star Wars*[39] movies.

Earlier I said that I believed in a Godly creation. Satan has been working hard to destroy this creation because of his fall from heaven. When early man and woman were created, Satan deceived them into thinking they could ignore God's instructions.[40] Their mistake separated them from God and left the rest of all humans that follow, to inherit their mistakes as far as God was concerned.[41] They exercised their independence from God's instructions by being selfish. When Jesus came, died, and lived again, he paid the price for their mistakes and through Him; we regain communication and friendship with God. Satan is working hard to destroy this relationship. Why, you might ask?

When Jesus returns to take the God-seekers to heaven, and the rest are sent to hell, Satan and his followers will also be sent to an eternal torture called the lake of fire or hell.[42] Satan's plan is to rob God of as many of the God-seekers as possible. The closer it gets to the return of Jesus, the more effort Satan will place on preventing the God-seekers from finding God and robbing God of his creation.

This is important to remember, because of my second statement. The devious schemes of Satan are so sinister, that some of those who seek God, said the redemptive prayer, and have not continuously studied, prayed, and sought God, will be deceived and destroyed. According to Matthew, 24:13; *"But those who endure to the end will be saved."* If you're saying to yourself—*"What, this can't be true?"*—Then you're not alone.

In Second Corinthians 4:4 (NLT), the writer Paul gives us insight:

> *"Satan, the god of this evil world, has blinded the minds of those who don't believe, so they cannot see the glorious light of the Good News* (Jesus) *that is shining on them. They don't understand the message we preach about the glory of Christ, who is the exact likeness of God."*

How it possible for Satan to be like this? He is a con artist. In the books, movies, and TV programs mentioned earlier, you will notice over the last 66 years, these media forms have been delivering specific messages. In the last 20 years, the messages have become stronger. The messages include; a) There are forces outside ourselves controlling us, b) Aliens are real, c) Hybrid people—a mixture of man and machine or men and aliens with special gifts—are good for us. Movies like *Star Wars*[43], *Avatar*[44], *Terminator*[45], *Independence Day*[46], *Men in Black*[47], are supposedly entertainment. TV programs like *Mork & Mindy*[48], *Third Rock*[49], *X-Files*[50], and a host of others are also family entertainment. Isn't this right?

How much TV and news time is dedicated to UFO activity and reports in recent years? Did you know the United Nations has appointed a special ambassador to be the representative for the world, when aliens land on earth? Confirmation of this information may be read in a CBS News article from September 27, 2010.[51]

Paranormal related movies, TV programs, and even cartoons for children, have flooded the mass-market in the last 10 years. Do you ever wonder why?

Here is another interesting piece of information. Did you know that Time Warner, Walt Disney, Viacom, News Corporation, CBS Corporation, and NBC Universal are the six entities that control almost everything we watch, hear, and read?[52] Hypothetically, what if the heads of these six entities gathered secretly and planned the dispersal of information. How much influence could they exert on the population?

I'm not saying this actually happened, or is even true, but I also believe there are evil forces at work, which are developing a long-range plan, a scheme of deception. Remember, the plan is to deceive God-seekers and the world, and to rob God of his creation.

In my research, I discovered that only 17 percent of the population *does not believe* aliens and UFOs exist, 48 percent *are not sure* if extraterrestrial life exists, and 36 percent *are convinced aliens exist.*[53] Given these statistics, it's easy to hypothesize on possible reasons the media is working the three messages listed earlier: Outside forces control us, aliens are real, and hybrid people are good.[54] We must be prepared for the coming deceptions, to remain true God-seekers. But, why?

The following statement is my theory. It is an example of how we can be deceived into accepting and adopting erroneous information. I have no proof, this only a hypothetical idea, but aliens, who could be fallen angels, will show up on earth as aliens. We greet them with open arms. They say they created us and because our planet is dying (that is, global warming, wars and conflicts, famines, terrorist plots) they are here to save their creation. They further tell us that our history was provided to certain individuals to write down over the course of thousands of years—like our Bible. They'll say the idea of God was theirs, as a way of giving us hope for a future. Finally, yet importantly, they'll say that for the last 66 years, they have been abducting people to create alien-human hybrid people and many of them are living among us already. Doesn't this sound like a plausible movie plot?

How many of you reading this, felt like nodding in agreement with my statement. How many of you think this information could be true? If we look at the statistics listed earlier, anywhere between 50 to 84 percent of the people today could accept my theory as true. This is one form of a great deception, or a lie to rob you from God. We must be defensive God-seekers by avoiding deceptions to survive our journey. Second Corinthians 11:13–15 (NLT), explains how the deception works:

> *"These people are false apostles. They have fooled you by disguising themselves as apostles of Jesus. But I am not surprised! Even Satan can disguise himself as an angel of light. So it is no wonder his servants can also do it by pretending to be godly ministers. In the end, they will get every punishment their wicked deeds deserve."*

Everything I've written in this chapter of my book only skims the surface of information we need to read and digest. You'll find many of the answers you're seeking in the Bible. By preparing yourself for the possible deceptions and continuing to seek God, are just a few of the things that will protect you on your journey to understand God. The next chapter will lay out a plan to guide and assist you in your search for more answers.

Just remember, if the enemy can convince you that your ideas about life, match those of the other people around you, and convinces you that your own path is what God wants, this is the start of serious trouble. A reality check occurs when we read Proverbs 14:12 (GNT); *"What you think is the right road may lead to death."*

The following new prayer will prepare us on our journey for the truth. Please join me by reading this aloud:

God, thank You for hearing the words I'm reading. Thank You for sending Your Angels to watch over and protect me. I'm glad You are in my life because You have forgiven me for my failures. You are opening new doors of truth for me and providing wisdom so I can understand what I read in the Bible. Teach me how to pray, and provide me with other God-seekers, like myself, to join me on my journey for the truth. Protect me from anything evil and grant me wisdom to decide who is evil or good. I want to continue seeking You and I love You, because You first loved me.

Reviewing this Chapter

List some ways that you can learn how to walk defensively through your journey.

_____

_____

_____

_____

_____

_____

_____

How have deceptions in your life derailed you from your goals?

_____

_____

_____

_____

_____

_____

_____

When the deceptions in your life are exposed, how does this make you feel?

_____

_____

_____

_____

_____

_____

_____

_____

Chapter 9

Culture Shock

I'm a person who normally doesn't trust others much. In fact, I believed for most of my life, that if you wanted something done right, you did it yourself. Unfortunately, this attitude of self-reliance isn't friendly with other people. But, I am now learning to release my self-reliant nature and beginning to trust God for direction in my life.

This by no means suggests that I sit for hours in the lotus position, pondering the lint in my navel, until some Divine message thumps me on the head. At the same time, God's messages delivered to me can sometimes take a long time—even years—and often it won't be super clear. If I am to grow as a God-seeker, I must wait and listen to God.

This is why reading God's words are so helpful. Not just the Bible either, there are books of old that are considered divinely inspired, but not included in our current Bibles. Some of these books were written before Jesus and some after. Works like the Book of Enoch, the Book of Jasher, and the writings of Josephus are just some examples. Occasionally, the Bible refers to these other books, even though they weren't included in the scriptures. I'll go one-step further; there are books written today, and offered in bookstores, that are also God inspired. Many hold important ideas and lessons for us. Reading is important to our journey and we will find God's messages for us if we seek them out.

Another important step in our God-seeking journey is learning to pray. You'll notice that several prayers have been included in this book and these will help you learn to communicate with God. If you're going to be friends with God, then talk with Him. How many times do you text or email one of your friends? By the way, there's no monthly service charge or a limit on the number of times you can communicate with God—He's unlimited.

If you had a garden and watered only half the rows every month, but the other half every other day, what would be the result? Provided the one side watered so rarely didn't wilt and expire, you'd notice a difference in the growth and crop produced. It's no different for you, if you don't invest time in being with other people like yourself—who've decided to seek God—then your experience will be like the poorly watered rows of your garden.

The importance of being around other God-seekers, who are learning about God, praying, and reading God's words, cannot be ignored. Imagine if no one called, sent a text, emailed, or sent you a card on your birthday. How would you feel? Granted, if you're over a certain age, this analogy might seem a bit ridiculous, but when people do remember your birthday, how does it make you feel? Being social with other God-seekers is the same thing. It encourages and motivates us.

Like the garden analogy I used, what you feed your brain will affect your development along your journey. This includes the music we listen to, the movies we watch, and the kinds of friends with whom we associate. All of these things have an influence on our journey, and it may require adjustments in our life. King David wrote his words of advice in Psalms 1:1–6 (GNT):

> *"Happy are those who reject the advice of evil people, who do not follow the example of sinners or join those who have no use for God. Instead, they find joy in obeying the Law of the Lord, and they study it day and night. They are like trees that grow beside a stream, that bear fruit at the right time, and whose leaves do not dry up. They succeed in everything they do. But evil people are not like this at all; they are like straw the wind blows away. Sinners will be condemned by God and kept apart from God's own people. The righteous are guided and protected by the Lord, but the evil are on the way to their doom."*

As we mingle with other God-seekers, you may find that they are called by many different names like Christians (to be Christ-like), believers, followers of Christ, servants of the Lord, Disciples of Christ, Jesus People, and Apostles. I'm using the name "God-seeker" in this book. I chose this name in an effort to avoid using labels. Some people may find it uncomfortable or may get their defenses up, when certain labels are attached, so I chose God-seeker. For example, when I read about ministers who abuse children and run mega-churches fueled by vast sums of money for their own benefit, I don't want to identify my God-seeking journey with their behavior. Instead, I want to be around other God-seekers like myself.

Deciding on where to go and be around other God-seekers can be tough. For me I reduce it to two simple questions:

1) When the group I visit follows what I've learned in the Bible— that's good.
2) When they teach things that make me cringe, or worry— that's bad.

As you continue on your journey, you may discover the group you originally joined isn't a good fit. That's okay, keep looking. It may happen quickly or take time, but always evaluate what they're teaching you with what you read in the Bible. Pray and ask God, He will help you in your search as well. One of the first things you'll notice when you join a group is their language. They speak in phrases they've heard or learned. It may sound like a foreign language.

As a result, our journey may leave us feeling as if we're entering a foreign county. At times, the direction we're headed on journey will seem confusing. There are outside influences that will hinder or help us on our journey, including our social interactions. Being aware of our surroundings will benefit our growth as God-seekers and limit the opportunity for failures (and our failures may lead to depression).

I remember when I first moved to Germany many years ago. I barely spoke a few words of their language. Their culture, social ideals, and society were foreign. I experienced culture shock. But, after many years living there, complete strangers would walk up to me, and in German would ask me for directions or information. After answering their questions, they thanked me and continued as if everything were normal. When I left Germany eight years later, most people could not tell I was an American.

I experienced a greater culture shock during my first visit to Japan for business years later. With blond hair and being at least a foot taller than the average Japanese citizen, I could not blend into their society because of my appearance. I knew little of their language and could not read their signs. Once I got on the wrong train and found myself lost, and miles from my destination. I was on the verge of panic when small schoolchildren noticed my panicked expression and they figured out I was lost. They kindly spoke their version of English, guiding me to the correct train, and helped me reach my destination. The overwhelming satisfaction of being assisted left me drained emotionally. When you join a group of God-seekers, you may encounter similar culture shock equal to these experiences.

Do not be discouraged, but ask the group you've joined to explain their choice of words. You might even ask if they could explain what they're saying, but in their own terminology. Throughout this book, I've worked hard to avoid the pitfall of using language commonly found among church attending people. I feel if I hadn't taken the time to do it this way, the words I chose would become an obstacle, and the book may be dismissed by the reader.

The following story indicates a couple of important points for us as God-seekers. The first point is that God knows who we are (Jesus had never met the person in this story before). The second point is we may need to move out of our comfort zone to hear the truth God is trying to tell us. Third, like Jesus, we should learn to speak in plain language and not code words or catch phrases learned through church.

To preface this story I'll explain some background details. Social influence during the time of Jesus was no different from ours. Certain social groups didn't associate with others and reading about it in the Bible, it reminds me of segregation in America from the late 1800s.

Now the story. In John 4:1–26 (GNT) we read where Jesus was traveling and came upon a well. The town where he stopped was not Hebrew, but Samarian. Hebrews and Samarians avoided all contact with each other. Jesus was tired and thirsty when a woman from town showed up to fill her container with water. Jesus asked her for a drink.

Not only did Jesus break cultural barriers (a Hebrew in contact with a Samarian), he crossed social barriers by speaking directly to a woman with whom he had no relationship. The woman could see Jesus was a Hebrew, so she said that she was flabbergasted that he would ask a Samarian woman for a drink of water. During their discussions, Jesus asked if the woman would bring her husband to the well so Jesus could meet the man. She said she had no husband. Then, Jesus said to her:

> *"You are right when you say you don't have a husband. You have been married to five men, and the man you live with now is not really your husband. You have told me the truth."*[55]

Jesus spoke respectfully to the woman at the well. The lesson here is that when we gather as God-seekers, we must be careful to avoid alienating new seekers by the phrases and language we use. Imagine being at a social gathering where most of the people are computer geeks, but you're not. The divide between you and the other people will be obvious and may create embarrassment. Using Jesus as an example, we will benefit other God-seekers and ourselves when we reach out to people with words they can associate with and recognize.

While I was in Germany, I experienced other culture shock issues. Because I was working for an American firm, I was granted the normal American holidays. On one particular day off, I decided to wash my car since the weather was unusually warm. While finishing my project, the German Police (Polezi) stopped for a visit. It seems I was visibly working during a German National and Religious holiday. In the area I lived, this was verboten (not allowed). I had no idea the American holiday coincided with the German religious holiday. I was then issued a citation, which I was able to have dismissed later, but the original penalty was 150 Deutsch Marks or about $50 US dollars. Understanding the God-seeker culture requires we remain sensitive to our surroundings.

As God-seekers, being aware of those around us is important, because we never know who is watching. Recently, the pastor of the church I attend delivered a teaching on how much God loves us. At the conclusion, he asked us an excellent question, and one that I think clarifies my point. His question: *"Do other people see in you, how much God loves them?"*

Living in Germany, I often saw other Americans whose conduct didn't represent all Americans. Without consideration, these individuals acted in ways that displayed a poor attitude toward our host country. Oddly, the Germans sitting with me would quietly complain about the expressed bravado, brash, and loud outbursts. It's important to note that our behavior as God-seekers can worsen cultural differences and alienate new potential God-seekers.

When around other God-seekers, you may have similar experiences because not every person who declares himself or herself a God-seeker walks a perfect life. Being human, we make mistakes—some deliberate, some not. It's easy to be critical and judge, but as stated earlier in Luke 6:41, (NKJ):

> *"And why do you look at the speck in your brother's eye, but do not notice the plank in your own eye?"*

This doesn't mean you should ignore the person's behavior, but there are clear instructions in the chapter of Galatians 6:1–5 (GNT) which teaches us how to deal with behaviors that create obstacles along our journey:

> *"My friends, if someone is caught in any wrongdoing, those of you who are spiritual should set him right; but you must do it in a gentle way. And keep an eye on yourselves, so you will not be tempted, too. Help carry one another's burdens, and in this way you will obey the law of Christ. If you think you are something when you are nothing, you are only deceiving yourself. You should each judge your own conduct. If it is good, then you can be proud of what you yourself have done, without having to compare it with what someone else has done. For each of you have to carry your own load."*

Being a God-seeker may seem daunting at first, but it does get easier as your journey progresses. This chapter of my book only covered the highlights, but important steps along your path. Earlier I mentioned the enemy, Satan, wants to rob you from God. In the next chapters, we will discover what Satan will try to cause your failure. In addition, why you must know and understand this enemy.

Some days, your journey will seem effortless; other days will appear as if the whole world is against you. This experience is normal, and anyone who tells you differently, is not being honest with you. In fact, James 1:12–13 (GNT) says this:

> *"Happy are those who remain faithful under trials, because when they succeed in passing such a test, they will receive as their reward the life which God has promised to those who love him. If we are tempted by such trials, we must not say, 'This temptation comes from God.' For God cannot be tempted by evil, and he tempts no one."*

Even Jesus, who was perfect, endured troubled days and battled Satan. We'll soon learn what Jesus did to deal with the enemy. His life is an example for us, which is why people who are trying to be like Christ Jesus, call themselves Christians.

As usual, and by now you must be getting used to this, I have a new prayer for us to read aloud:

> *God, thank You for hearing the words I'm reading. Thank You for placing Your Angels around to watch and protect me. Teach me to love and forgive other people, because You love and have forgiven me. You are in my life and I rejoice. Thank you for Your wisdom and answering my prayers. Protect me from the enemy and do not let him rob me from You. I will continue to seek You because I am reading Your words and they will guide me on my journey for truth.*

Reviewing this Chapter

Have you ever traveled to a foreign country or been in a group situation where you were the minority in the room? How did it make you feel?

_____

_____

_____

_____

_____

_____

_____

Has there ever been a time in your life when something you said or did, and thought no one was listening or watching, yet it was revealed later? How did this revelation make you feel?

_____

_____

_____

_____

_____

_____

_____

Chapter 10

The Road Less Traveled

Our God-seeker journey involves many decisions, which will have both positive and negative influences. Not unlike a walk in the woods or a camping trip, each decision we make can affect our safety and enjoyment. To explain this I'll use an example from my past to highlight my point.

Being outdoors and in the woods can invoke feelings of peace and calm—provided one doesn't get lost while out there. For a brief period of my life, I was involved with the Sierra Club because of my love for the outdoors. This organization has service trips offered around the world. At one's own expense, the trips involve spending weekends to upwards of a month working on things for the environment.

I took part in several weekend service trips and two weeklong trips while a member of the Sierra Club. The last trip I served on was in the Gila Mountains of New Mexico. After packing everything needed for the week onto our backs, the group of 40-some individuals ranging in various ages, climbed steep peaks and hiked into deep valleys.

The journey was worth the effort, because eight hours later we arrived at our camp beside a loud and cold river. That week, we repaired trails originally opened by the CCC (Civilian Conservation Corps) during the late 1930s. It was hot, sweaty work, producing filthy worn-out individuals, who could barely lift a fork at evening mealtime. I loved it and met some great people.

Toward the end of the trip, we completed the tasks given to us by the National Park Service so everyone was given some free time. I decided to explore the trail we worked so hard on and reach the summit on the other side of our river valley. Several others joined me, but because we were exhausted, we chose our own pace. Twice, a thunderstorm flashed lightening and pounded the trail with rain, forcing us to dive for cover. I left a resting group during one pause to go forward alone.

As I neared the end of this trail on the summit, the path was not obvious from use because we had only opened the lower half of the trail on this service trip. It had been 40 years since this upper half of the trail had been used, requiring me to pick my way along looking for small clues. Once I reached the top, the views were fantastic and breathtaking. After resting, I decided to head back down since no one joined me. I'm slightly red-green colorblind, and had difficulty spotting the red plastic flags deposited by the Forest Service marking the trail among the green foliage. Trying to find the trail, I was confused several times needing to backtrack so I could find the original path.

The sun was setting and I became nervous, which made the situation worse. I had to fight panic feelings by remembering to remain calm, from the training I received as a former Boy Scout. Eventually I made my way back to a more familiar trail, and there I met some young men who were out looking for me. That evening I reflected on the path I chose that day, the one traveled by few.

As a God-seeker, picking your way through the journey for the truth, the path you choose may seem traveled by few individuals. It's easy to get lost, feel alone, and miss the clues showing where the trail leads. Sometimes, panic may set in, with fear and worry about what's next. This is why prayer and reading God's words are so helpful, because His words will provide guidance on the journey—like a map of sorts. The answer to nearly everything we face as humans can be found in God's words within the Bible.

The difficulty with your journey could relate to the fact that few people choose the road less traveled, and they become easily discouraged. A rich man once approached Jesus asking what he must do to get into heaven. Jesus told the man to obey the Ten Commandments. The rich man replied that from a young age he had followed the commandments. In Luke 18:22–25 (GNT) Jesus then gave the rich man new instructions:

> "'There is still one more thing you need to do. Sell all you have and give the money to the poor, and you will have riches in heaven; then come and follow me.' But when the man heard this, he became sad, because he was rich. Jesus saw that he was sad and said, 'How hard it is for rich people to enter the Kingdom of God! It is much harder for a rich person to enter the Kingdom of God than for a camel to go through the eye of a needle.'"

Jesus understood the rich man enough to know he obeyed all the commandments, but he also knew that this man's wealth would prevent him from entering heaven. If as God-seekers we allow our priorities to supersede God's instructions, we run the risk of losing the path and getting lost.

This is what happened in my life when I allowed my own selfish desires to rule my judgments and control my decisions. God didn't change his mind; he simply gave me the free-will choice to make up my own path.

The other important lesson in this story about the rich man is Jesus's comment about the "eye of the needle." If you're thinking about seeing a camel going through a sewing needle eye, this task does seem impossible. However, as mentioned earlier, Jesus used parables to show the message he was trying to teach, and parables were always relevant. Jesus knew that on the walls of each city were gates that closed in the evening to keep marauders and bandits out. At the bottom of the eastern gate was a small opening, just large enough for a man to squeeze through.

If a traveler was locked out of the city because the gates were closed, they could crawl through the tight opening at the bottom of the gate. As the sun was setting and the gates were shut, the sunlight shining through the opening looked like a needle. Most times, the travelers were riding on camels, carrying large packs.

If the gates were locked, the traveler would unpack his belongings, shove them through the small opening, and then with much effort force the camel through the eye-opening of the gate. This process could take hours and the traveler risked having their belongings stolen in the process. Travelers would beat the camel with a rod until they forced the camel through the tight opening, because being outside the walls meant being robbed and or killed.

The people around Jesus knew this information and understood the difficulty of getting a camel through the "eye of the needle." Although this was an exhausting and challenging task, it was not impossible. Nonetheless, this thing with the camel is easier versus a rich man getting into heaven. The people understood Jesus's meaning.

The path we choose as God-seekers may seem impossible, but Jesus spoke to those standing nearby when they inquired about dealing with such impossibilities; *"Jesus answered, 'What is humanly impossible is possible for God.'"* Luke 18:27 (GNT)

Sometimes, when we are directed down the path traveled by few, we feel alone. We may even resist because we don't understand God's logic. Jonah in the Bible was such a man that resisted taking an illogical path at God's insistence. In the Old Testament, Jonah 1:1–3 (GNT), it explains Jonah's rebellion:

> *"One day the Lord spoke to Jonah son of Amittai. He said, 'Go to Nineveh, that great city, and speak out against it; I am aware of how wicked its people are.' Jonah, however, set out in the oppo- site direction to get away from the Lord. He went to Joppa, where he found a ship about to go to Spain. He paid his fare and went aboard with the crew to sail to Spain, where he would be away from the Lord."*

The idea of rebelling against God's instructions isn't new. Jonah lived several thousand years ago, but human nature hasn't changed. God wanted Jonah to take the path traveled by few, but Jonah had other ideas. The journey Jonah chose didn't go well, and this is a huge under- statement. A storm blew in and threatened to capsize the ship Jonah was riding. The crew feared for their lives and began throwing the cargo overboard to make the ship lighter. Meanwhile, Jonah was sound asleep in the lower cargo hold. When the crew found Jonah, they demanded he get up and pray to his God so the crew might be saved.

When praying didn't work, they eventually drew straws to find who might be responsible for their predicament. Jonah pulled the short straw and immediately they interrogated Jonah to find out why he was the cause of their trouble.

In Jonah1:9–17 (GNT) the story continues:

> *"'I am a Hebrew,' Jonah answered. 'I worship the Lord, the God of heaven, who made land and sea.' Jonah went on to tell them that he was running away from the Lord. The sailors were terrified, and said to him, 'That was an awful thing to do!' The storm was getting worse all the time, so the sailors asked him, 'What should we do to you to stop the storm?' Jonah answered, 'Throw me into the sea, and it will calm down. I know it is my fault that you are caught in this violent storm.' Instead, the sailors tried to get the ship to shore, rowing with all their might. But the storm was becoming worse and worse, and they got nowhere. So they cried out to the Lord, 'O Lord, we pray, don't punish us with death for taking this man's life! You, O Lord, are responsible for all this; it is your doing.' Then they picked Jonah up and threw him into the sea, and it calmed down at once. This made the sailors so afraid of the Lord that they offered a sacrifice and promised to serve him. At the Lord's command a large fish swallowed Jonah, and he was inside the fish for three days and three nights."*

In the beginning of this book, I mentioned how I started on the path to the truth, was sidetracked, started down the path again, and then lost my way. All along this journey, God was trying to get my attention, but I was headstrong and thought I knew better. When I finally gave up my control freak nature and gave God my heart, my mind, my body (everything 100%), this is when I discovered the information I had been missing. I was trying to run my journey my way and only call on God in difficult times. But God wanted me to communicate with Him all the time, not just when I was in trouble.

If you have trouble understanding God's logic, I suggest you read the rest of Jonah's story. His rebellion didn't end with being swallowed by the fish, but you'll need to finish reading Jonah's story to understand how far a man can push God, and still be loved by his creator.

At one point, Jonah even screams at God telling him; *"I am better-off dead than alive."* When we rebel against God, we become desperate, hopeless, depressed, and wish for death. But, death should never be an option.

The road less traveled is narrow and sometimes difficult. When you feel discouraged, read God's words, because they will encourage you on your journey for the truth. Many places in the Bible offer words of encouragement and other God-seekers will also share what they've found to be helpful. My favorite verse is Isaiah 40:28–31 (GNT):

> *"Don't you know? Haven't you heard? The Lord is the everlasting God; he created all the world. He never grows tired or weary. No one understands his thoughts. He strengthens those who are weak and tired. Even those who are young grow weak; young people can fall exhausted. But those who trust in the Lord for help will find their strength renewed. They will rise on wings like eagles; they will run and not get weary; they will walk and not grow weak."*

This Bible verse reminds us of several promises: 1) God is always there for us, 2) God never gets tired, 3) you will get discouraged and want to quit, and 4) if you wait for and follow God's instructions, you'll soar like an eagle.

On the destructive side is the enemy (Satan and his team) who will exploit your weaknesses. If money drives you to excel, this could become an obstacle causing you to have wrong priorities. Anytime we allow our wants to guide our thinking, it's a guarantee that God will pull back and let us run our own course. I did this for most of my life, and the results were hugely disappointing. As a self-sufficient person, the enemy exploited my weaknesses and drew me away from God.

It's important to remember that Satan's only goal is **to rob you from God**. When making choices for your life, if you filter every decision through that knowledge, the direction you need to take will become easier. Before each decision, ask yourself:

> *If I chose this, will it give the enemy the opportunity of robbing me from God?*

Reviewing this Chapter

Have you ever made a choice that seemed to go against everyone's recommendations? What was the outcome?

_____

_____

_____

_____

_____

_____

_____

Can you describe a time in your life when nothing was going right? What were the results?

_____

_____

_____

_____

_____

_____

_____

Chapter 11

The Thief

Since Satan's goal is to rob us from God, it's important we understand how he carries out this objective. His chief weapon is deception. When depressed, my deception was thinking I didn't matter and that my life was useless. Would it surprise you to learn that the beginning of my deception came from Satan? He will use other people, books, movies, the internet—anything to deceive you into thinking his way. Satan is like a lawyer who presents half-truths, partial information, and twists the language around so that juries, and you, are fooled.

What's interesting is that anytime someone mentions the devil or Satan, the immediate imagery we visualize is a red monster with horns on his head, a long tail, and holding a pitchfork. Thank you Hollywood, but it's not even close to the truth. Since Satan is God-seeker's enemy, it's important we understand who this enemy is. We find an accurate picture of Satan in the Bible. Originally, Satan was an archangel called Lucifer. In Ezekiel 28:12–17 (GNT) God describes this angel:

> *"You were once an example of perfection. How wise and handsome you were! You lived-in Eden, the garden of God, and wore gems of every kind: rubies and diamonds; topaz, beryl, carnelian, and jasper; sapphires, emeralds, and garnets. You had ornaments of gold. They were made for you on the day you were created. I put a terrifying angel there to guard you. You lived on my holy mountain (heaven) and walked among sparkling gems. Your conduct was perfect from*

the day you were created until you began to do evil. You were busy buying and selling, and this led you to violence and sin. So I forced you to leave my holy mountain, and the angel who guarded you drove you away from the sparkling gems. You were proud of being handsome, and your fame made you act like a fool. Because of this, I hurled you to the ground and left you as a warning to other kings."

According to the Bible, Lucifer stood 12 cubits (a cubit is 18") so his height was an astounding 18 feet. He was big and important. After Satan's fall, Jesus called him the *"father of lies"* and in Second Corinthians 11:14 (GNT) Paul warns us; *"Well, no wonder! Even Satan can disguise himself to look like an angel of light!"* This doesn't match the Hollywood description, does it?

The following is a Bible shortlist of names this evil enemy is called. It is by no means complete. There are references in the Bible for each name. Some of these are easily recognized because you've seen them in books, movies, and on TV programs. If you're wondering why I devoted so much space to this character, it's **because Satan wants to rob you from God and will fiercely work toward that goal**. I cannot stress enough, the importance of seeing Satan for who he is. Here is the shortlist:

666 (Revelation 13:18)
Abaddon or Destroying Angel (Revelation 9:11)
Accuser of the Brethren (Revelation 12:10)
Adversary (First Peter 5:8),
Angel of Light (Second Corinthians 11:14)
Angel of the Bottomless Pit and Ruler of the Darkness (Revelations 9:11)
Anointed cherub (Ezekiel 28:14)
Antichrist (First John 4:3)
Baal (Romans 11:4)
Balaam the False Teacher (Jude 1:11)
The Beast (Revelation 14:9–10)
Beelzebub (Matthew 12:24, 27 & Mark 3:22 & Luke 11:15, 18–19)
Belial (Second Corinthians 6:15)
Blasphemer of God (Revelation 13:1)

Chief or Prince of Demons (Luke 11:15)
The Viper (Isaiah 14:29, 59:5)
Deceiver (Revelation 12:9)
Devil (Matthew 4:1–11, 9:33, 11:18, 12:22, 13:29, 15:22, 17:18, 25:41
    & Mark 5:15–18, 7:26–30 & Luke 4:2–13, 4:33–35, 7:33, 8:12,
    8:29, 9:42, 11:14 & John 6:70, 7:20, 8:44–52, 10:20–21, 13:2 &
    Acts 10:38 13:10 & Ephesians 4:27, 6:11 & First Timothy 3:6–7 &
    Second Timothy 2:26 & Hebrews 2:14 & James 4:7 & First Peter
    5:8 & First John 3:8–10 & Jude 1:9 & Revelation 2:10, 12:9, 12:12,
    20:2, 20:10)
Enemy or Adversary (Matthew 13:39)
Evil One (John 17:15)
False Light (First John 2:8)
Father of Lies (John 8:44)
God of this World or Ruler of the Night (Second Corinthians 4:4)
God (Revelation 20:8)
King of Babylon (Isaiah 14:4)
King of Tyrus or Tyre (Ezekiel 28:12)
Leviathan (Isaiah 27:1)
Lucifer or the Bright and Morning Star (Isaiah 14:12–14)
Man of Sin (Second Thessalonians 2:3–4)
Perdition (Second Thessalonians 2:3)
Power of Darkness (Colossians 1:13–14)
Prince of this World (John 12:31–32, 14:30, 16:11 & First Corinthians
    2:6–8)
Satan (First Chronicles 21:1 & Job 1:6–12, 2:1–7 & Psalm 109:6 &
    Zechariah 1:3:1–2 & Matthew 4:10, 12:26, 16:23 & Mark 1:13,
    3:23–26, 4:15, 8:33 & Luke 4:8, 10:18, 11:18, 13:16, 22:3, 22:31 &
    John 13:27 & Acts 5:3, 26:18 & Romans 16:20 & First Corinthians
    5:5, 7:5 & Second Corinthians 2:11, 11:14 & First Thessalonians
    2:18 & Second Thessalonians 2:9 & First Timothy 1:20, 5:15 &
    Revelation 2:9, 2:13, 2:24, 3:9; 12:9, 20:2, 20:7)
Impostor (First Timothy 4:1)
Tempter (Matthew 4:3)
Thief (Matthew 24:43 & Luke 12:39 & John 10:10)
Wormwood (Revelation 8:11)

I've just listed the names of our enemy Satan, but we must understand that his goal is to rob us from God. He will use depression as a means to destroy you—God's creation. The first example of Satan working to rob God of his creation can be found in the book of Genesis of the Bible. Anytime a painter or sculptor depicts this scene from the Bible, they show a naked woman holding an apple and a large snake taunting her. Satan is an evil spirit and he will change into any form he wishes, including an angel of light, because he's a deceiver.

Satan took the form of a snake (a.k.a. serpent or viper) when he pushed Eve to eat from the tree that she and Adam were restricted from touching. Serpents must have had arms and legs at the time, because when God found out what Satan had done, he cursed the snake. Genesis 3:14 (GNT) tell us:

> "Then the Lord God said to the snake, 'You will be punished for this; you alone of all the animals must bear this curse: From now on you will crawl on your belly, and you will have to eat dust as long as you live.'"

This thief will do anything to achieve his goal of robbing God. If anything sexual has a strong attraction for you, Satan will convince you that God would approve of you watching internet porn, because it doesn't hurt anyone. If being in charge of things or being a leader is your desire, Satan will convince you that God wants strong leaders who are self-reliant and must take charge. Satan is a thief and his goal is to rob God.

At the end of a long 40-day fasting and prayer session, Satan tried using his tricks on Jesus. In Matthew 4:3–10 (GNT) it says that Jesus was hungry, and:

> "Then the Devil came to him (Jesus) and said, 'If you are God's Son, order these stones to turn into bread.' But Jesus answered, 'The scripture says, "Human beings cannot live on bread alone, but need every word that God speaks."' Then the Devil took Jesus to Jerusalem, the Holy City, set him on the highest point of the Temple, and said to him, 'If you are God's Son, throw yourself down, for the scripture

says, "God will give orders to his angels about you; they will hold you up with their hands, so not even your feet will be hurt on the stones."' Jesus answered, 'But the scripture also says, "Do not put the Lord your God to the test."' Then the Devil took Jesus to a very high mountain and showed him all the kingdoms of the world in all their greatness. 'All this I will give you,' the Devil said, 'if you kneel down and worship me.' Then Jesus answered, 'Go away, Satan! The scripture says, "Worship the Lord your God and serve only him!"'

Satan tried three times to rob Jesus from God. He attacked him while he was weak and tired, plus Satan used quotes from the Bible to fight against Jesus. First, Satan appealed to the hunger needs of Jesus. When that didn't work, he tempted Jesus by having him prove his Godly power. Then finally, Satan appealed to Jesus's love for saving humankind, but the enemy failed. If you read the same account in Luke 4:13 (GNT) it says; *"When the Devil finished tempting Jesus in every way, he left him for a while."* This is like the movie *Terminator*[56], when the evil character taunts his victims by saying; *"I'll be back."*

The enemy does not give up. **His goal is to rob you from God**, and he has no remorse about his methods. Given the information in this chapter of my book, whenever I see someone trying to communicate with the devil, I want to escape from the room screaming, as if my hair is on fire. Everything related to the enemy results in death and separation from God.

Before writing this book, the circumstances of my life were dictated through depression and it ruled my thoughts daily. Like rose-colored glasses, everything that occurred in my life was filtered through my depression. I was convinced God hated me and was punishing me, but I was sadly mistaken. My old pattern was to scold myself constantly for my failures. When I realized that I could do nothing to earn God's love or forgiveness, it was a new step to a breakthrough in my depression. God's love just is! And, His love was established long before our birth. When we ask God to forgive us, the Bible tells us that our mistakes are removed as far as the East is from the West.[57]

One can travel North Pole to South Pole and back, but if you travel east, you will never meet the west, and vice versa. Once I understood sin removal, regarding my failures before God, then I could understand how God sees me. My mistakes are removed as far as the east is from the west (nonexistent) and replaced by God's pure love. Satan was using my depression to keep me in prison mentally and away from God.

The fastest way that Satan wins at robbing us from God is through deception. He will find us when we are sad or depressed and begin feeding us lies, telling us suicide is a way to be free. Satan was using this deception on me and it was a daily battle.

How do we fight this enemy? We follow the example of Jesus by reading God's words, communicating with God, and associating ourselves with other God-seekers. When it feels like the assaults are overwhelming, we call other God-seekers and they will pray for and with us. When the thoughts of suicide and the voices inside our head are telling us that death is the answer, God's words will prevail. How you ask?

"And I (Jesus) will be with you always..." Matthew 28:20 (GNT)

"I (Jesus) will never leave you; I will never abandon you." Hebrews 13:5 (GNT)

"For I am certain that nothing can separate us from God's love: neither death nor life, neither angels nor other heavenly rulers or powers, neither the present nor the future, neither the world above nor the world below – there is nothing in all creation that will ever be able to separate us from the love of God which is ours through Christ Jesus our Lord." Romans 8:38–39 (GNT)

"The Lord is my shepherd; I have everything I need. He lets me rest in fields of green grass and leads me to quiet pools of fresh water. He gives me new strength. He guides me in the right paths, as He has promised. Even if I go through the deepest darkness, I will not be afraid, Lord, for you are with me. Your shepherd's rod and staff protect me. You prepare a banquet for me, where all my enemies can see me; You welcome me as an honored guest and fill my cup to the brim. I know that Your goodness and love will be with me all my life; and Your house will be my home as long as I live." Psalm 23:1–6 (GNT)

In this chapter, I've shared important aspects of the truth concerning God and His wishes for our life; how our enemy will do anything within his power to destroy us and our relationship with God. Earlier in my journey, I somehow missed this information, or at least the finer details, which is why I had to restart several times. Since I was self-reliant, I therefore felt responsible for the mess in my life. To end my pain I had to end my life, but that's not God's plan.

To clarify my point, the theme of this chapter can be reduced to three things:

1) God loves you more than you'll ever know
2) The enemy's goal is to rob you from God
3) Remember step one!

For the life of me, I cannot understand why certain individuals or churches have to make this message so complicated. Their list of rules, dos and don'ts, lead your focus away from these simple steps. If you understand step one, the concepts of suicide can only fit into the enemy's goal, and God loves you more than you'll ever know.

During Jesus's time on earth, he criticized the religious leaders (called Pharisees) because they were more interested in appearing saintly or respectable to society. Their hearts missed the above steps and they strutted around acting as if they were above everyone else— condescending and judgmental. Even when they prayed, it was to impress other people. The followers of Jesus asked him; *"Then how shall we pray?"*[58]

Jesus taught them a simple prayer that was to be a pattern on how we should pray to God. Prayer is our main tool against the enemy. This is why there are so many practical prayers listed in this book. Our success over the enemy's goal is communicating with God. So now I have a new prayer for you that is based on the one Jesus taught to those who followed His teachings. It is a powerful weapon against deceptions and our enemy.

Because some of us are so familiar with the "Lord's Prayer," I've changed the wording of this prayer. I did it because we must remember Jesus was only teaching a method of prayer, not that we should repeat something word for word. Reiterating the words of the "Lord's Prayer" repeatedly wasn't Jesus's intention. Jesus was teaching us how we should pray, a prayer template to show us an example.

Please pray with me and read the following words aloud, but remember this is only a guide to follow in your future prayers. Learn to use you own words when praying.

God, I know you listen to me when I pray and are delighted in my words. Your name and love are greater than anything I can think of. You've given me Angels to watch and protect me, because I give my mind, body, and soul to You. I hold nothing back from You. I may be capable of earning a living, buying food, and running my life, but every moment of my life I want to remember that I am Your creation, and You provided these things for me in the first place. I forgive those who have hurt me so I can receive forgiveness from You. Teach me to love people who injure me. Protect me from the enemy Satan and do not let him rob me from You. I know that I am now part of You and I will tell You everyday how happy this makes me. The earth and the stars will eventually be destroyed, but You and Your heaven will last forever. Amen

(By the way, Amen means – So be it, or make it so)

Reviewing this Chapter

Have you ever felt like a battle raged inside your head?

_____

_____

_____

_____

_____

_____

How did you deal with these thoughts in the past?

_____

_____

_____

_____

_____

_____

_____

Are you now aware that God loves you more than you will ever know?

_____

_____

_____

_____

_____

_____

_____

How does this make you feel?

_____

_____

_____

_____

_____

_____

_____

_____

Chapter 12

Future Prospects

Hurricane Katrina was the most destructive and perhaps deadliest hurricane of 2005.[59] Over 1,800 people lost their life because of this storm. In 2011, the Tōhoku earthquake in Japan and the following tsunami claimed the life of nearly 16,000 individuals. In 2004, the Indian Ocean earthquake and tsunami that followed claimed 280,000 lives as the waves spread over a 1,000 miles of shoreline, affecting many countries. Disasters such as these will sweep through an area and in a matter of minutes reduce entire towns to flattened rubbish.

Three years after the Katrina storm, I needed to fly to Florida and sell my mother's home. After packing her possessions and sending them along with the moving company, I drove her car across the south to her new home in Nevada.

During my trip, I arrived in New Orleans, Louisiana one morning and stopped at a fast-food restaurant for breakfast. Because of Katrina, entire neighborhoods were gone leaving only flat concrete and old large trees. For half a mile in every direction around the fast-food joint, there was nothing, just sand and concrete.

The once thriving community was gone. There were no homes, cars, streetlights, and no children playing in the street—just the lone newly rebuilt fast-food restaurant sitting in the very location it occupied before the disaster, that and a few scattered trees. Inside the restaurant hung pictures showing what the area looked like prior to the hurricane.

Sitting in my car eating, I surveyed the area and recognized the trees from the pictures, but everything else was gone.

Off in the distance sat a two-story building, nestled between large oaks, and resting on an outcrop of huge rocks. The building that sat atop the flat boulders was badly beaten, showing missing boards and ribs of the roof. Three years after the destructive storm, the owner was still working to repair his home. Debris littered the yard as he tossed damaged sections into piles and went about sawing and hammering. His home, although damaged, had survived.

In the New Testament chapter of Luke 6:47–49 (GNT), Jesus provided a similar illustration. Using plain language, Jesus was teaching the people who were gathered around about what is expected of us regarding God's words. Using a parable, Jesus said:

> *"Anyone who comes to Me and listens to My words and obeys them – I will show you what he is like. He is like a man who, in building his house, dug deep and laid the foundation on rock. The river flooded over and hit that house but could not shake it, because it was well built. But anyone who hears My words and does not obey them is like a man who built his house without laying a foundation; when the flood hit that house it fell at once – and what a terrible crash that was!"*

In this parable, the storm is the enemy, and we are the house. If we're communicating with God, studying His words, and spending time with other God-seekers, we resemble a house built on rocks.

While living on this earth and in our house, it's easy to be caught up ensuring we have a nice place and many things that give us pleasure. We like our big, flat-screen TVs, sound systems, and computers. These things are not bad in themselves, but we must remember that in an instant they can be removed with a storm, fire, earthquake, or stolen. These things are just stuff that makes living our life pleasurable.

In Philippians 3:8 (GNT), Paul tells us what our attitude should be concerning anything we consider necessary in this life:

> *"...I reckon everything as complete loss for the sake of what is so much more valuable, the knowledge of Christ Jesus my Lord.*

For his sake I have thrown everything away; I consider it all as mere garbage..."

Notice Paul didn't tell us to toss it all-out, he simply reminded us of what our attitude should be toward these things.

When I lost my home and many things I valued to my broken relationship, I grieved the loss. It represented so much effort, time, and money. I wanted God to punish the person responsible for my losses, and restore what was truly mine. It didn't work out that way. My possessions were getting in the way of a relationship with God. My hoarding was slow at first, but after 61 years, I had gathered many items I valued. I paid monthly fees to two storage units, as a legacy to my collection.

God wanted my attention, and so the circumstances of my life left me no choice but to start selling my belongings. I sold everything that I thought was important to me. I wanted nothing to prevent me from focusing on what God wanted for my life. I'm not saying you need to follow my example; this was just something I needed to do. Since I had lost my home, car, and job, it seemed like an easy step to sell my possessions. I wanted no anchors that would hold me back from my new journey.

Ten percent of everything I sold, I gave back to God. I was living on a limited income and struggling to survive, so the money from selling my personal items was helping me survive. I wasn't sure I could tithe (make an offering) to God at church because funds were tight, but I made the commitment anyway. God was changing my priorities. Despite my limited income, and thinking I could not afford to tithe, I manage to live each month comfortably.

Now every month I give this tithe first, before paying my bills. In the Old Testament, it tells us what will happen if we make this commitment to God. In Malachi 3:10 (GNT) God says this:

"Bring the full amount of your tithes to the church... Put me to the test and you will see that I will open the windows of heaven and pour out on you in abundance all kinds of good things."

I finally decided to give up worrying about the things I've lost, and started rejoicing about finding my way back to the truth. Currently, my journey is gaining momentum, and I can now look back and see how my life was before, versus how it's going now—I like 'now' a whole lot better.

One day during my scripture studies, I grabbed my Bible and it fell open to Joel in the Old Testament. I hadn't selected this section; I simply opened the Bible and started turning to the pages where I was reading last. When I looked down, I found Joel 2:25–26 (GNT):

> *"I will give you back what you lost in the years when swarms of locusts ate your crops. It was I, who sent this army against you. Now you will have plenty to eat, and be satisfied. You will praise the Lord your God, who has done wonderful things for you."*

Tears streamed down my face because I realized I had lost so much, but God had been behind the plans all along. I had been focusing on the wrong priorities. For me, new doors of truth were opening with each day. As long as I selfishly hoarded the personal things I valued, it would be like trying to grasp a fistful of sand. The tighter I squeezed the faster the sand ran out. By selling my stored possessions, I was opening my hand and letting the sand go. Matthew 6:33 (GNT) simplifies this lesson:

> *"Instead, be concerned above everything else with the Kingdom of God and with what he needs of you, and he will provide you with all these other things."*

From these experiences developed the concept (and the passion) for this book you're now reading. My wish is to share the truths I'm learning, in hope that you will benefit. Even if one person who reads this book undergoes the same change in his or her life—becoming a God-seeker like me—then it's been worth my candor on these pages.

When we started this journey together, I began by asking you to keep an open mind. I also asked you to keep your plans on hold. We discussed giving meaning to your life that God created us, and He gave us His words in the Bible to read. Even though we live in a society where we can microwave something to eat in minutes, life is a systematic process.

We talked about the difficulty of life. How we will often feel alone. It's at these moments when our anger rises to the surface, causing us to lash out at anything and everyone around us. However, God provides us with a solution that requires us to have a belief system or faith.

We also learned that God loves us so much, that He sent His Son Jesus, and our faults are covered through the sacrifice of Jesus on the cross.

We found out that the Day of Judgment is coming and the earth will be destroyed. Our struggle to survive in the meantime will be the result of Satan trying to attack us. If we are to survive, it will involve us spending time with other God-seekers, communicating with God through prayer, and studying His words.

I explained that when we first become God-seekers, it will seem like we're living in a foreign country. We may feel alone sometimes, but God is always with us and He never gives up on us. The most important lesson I've shared is that the enemy in our journey is Satan and his goal is to steal us from God. However, God loves us more than we will ever know.

Finally, I feel compelled to share with you one more personal story. This is a story that developed when my cousin Chuck was dying of cancer. Recently, I found the eulogy I delivered at his funeral service and I feel it best summarizes our human God-seeking experience.

When I visited with Chuck, the Wednesday before he passed away, his declining condition stunned me. A flood of emotions washed over me, including anger. After returning home, I sat in my living room staring straight ahead and had a long talk with God about how I'd do things if this were up to me.

I explained to God that there are grievous individuals on the daily news that could die—but not Chuck—he's given so much, and has done so many wonderful things. I asked God; *"Why on earth, do you have to make life so puzzling?"*

I looked up and sitting on my bookcase in front of me was a puzzle that Chuck had made years earlier. It was a wooden fish cut out into puzzle pieces. The individual cuts spelled out the letters J-E-S-U-S, or Jesus across the body of the fish. *"What are you telling me God? Are we supposed to make puzzle fish for Jesus, like Chuck?"*

Then it hit me what God was trying to reveal. Chuck was a collector of puzzles—so much, in fact, that it had become an obsession. In his home office sat a tall glass cabinet, a shrine for his puzzles. Nearly every nook and cranny was chocked full of wooden, paper, metal ring, and plastic puzzles. He even had that brainteaser block called the Rubik's Cube.

Remembering all of Chuck's puzzles, I realized that life can be puzzling and God was telling me that Chuck's collection was the answer to my simple question. Even though he was near death, Chuck was still being a minister to people. God was showing me that in fact, life is just like a jigsaw puzzle.

We are born and given a bag full of squiggly shapes and colors and told; *"This is your life, figure it out, put it together!"* The only problem is there isn't a box with a cute picture on the front to use as a guideline. We don't know what the whole picture is supposed to look like. In addition, the pieces of our life are not interchangeable with someone else.

Some puzzles are easy and have only a few pieces; others are more complex. Sometimes we're fortunate enough to have parents that go through the individual pieces looking for the ones with the straight edges, to form the frame of the puzzle. If we're lucky, by time were on our own, the frame is almost complete so that we have a foundation on which we can assemble the pieces of our lives. Others of us only get a portion of an edge, or perhaps a corner.

During our lives, we place pieces into the puzzle called life. Some pieces just drop right in, as if you knew just where to place them. Other times, we get frustrated while turning the piece repeatedly trying each edge—convinced it's the right place for this piece. We may even try to force the piece, by beating it into place with our fists.

Later on, the right piece does show up and we have to tear out the wrong piece to make room for the correct one. That's okay because God comes along and says not to worry. He has His healing clear tape of "love" to mend the broken piece, and some special glue called "grace" to patch the torn flap on another.

Often, we find ourselves working on a whole section of the puzzle that's not connected to anything else—out there hanging in the void. We wonder if it has anything to do with our life's puzzle. Then months, years go by; we may have even forgotten about that lonely section. Then out of nowhere, right in front of us sits these individual pieces, and we suddenly know exactly where they go. We say to ourselves, *hey, this connects that forgotten section, and wow, this all makes sense now. I can actually see my life coming together.*

We work and toil, forgetting the clock until one day God says; *"It's time."* Remember the days of school tests, and you're quickly filling in the answers, then someone calls out *"time."* In the grand scheme of things, those last few answers aren't really going to affect the outcome, but we frantically work on our puzzle, cramming pieces in where they shouldn't go, scrambling to finish.

Looking up at God, we plead. *"Please God, just a little more time. I know I can finish this, if you'll just give me a little more time. I know there are missing pieces, blank sections—okay, and perhaps too much tape and glue here and there—but I think I have a handle on this and can finish the job."*

That's when God smiles down at us and says; *"It's perfect; time to go."*

With His arm around our shoulder, He leads us to His home. The entire time, we're telling God how we needed more time, the whole thing is a mess, it's unfinished, there are missing pieces, broken pieces, mended and glued pieces, whole sections are still missing. We say to Him; *"In fact it was hard God, all those squiggly, jagged lines, the pieces all looked alike, there wasn't any picture on a box to go by. My puzzle really looks messy. Had I known, I would have straightened things up a bit, worked harder, I would have done more!"*

With that, God turns us around, smiles, and says; *"You see my child, where you saw jagged lines, broken pieces, missing sections, and a mess, I see something else."* Together we look up and see the jigsaw puzzle of our life.

"See there," says God. And, for a brief moment we do see; it's almost a complete picture of our life.

"From My vantage point," says God, *"I see only a perfect picture—no lines, no missing pieces, no broken pieces—from here I see a perfect picture of you and it's beautiful. Why, it's just as I imagined it!"*

When I allowed my depression to rule my thoughts and permitted the enemy to keep me away from God, I ran the risk of annihilating the colorful picture just described above. Suicide destroys God's vision for our lives and we rob God of His powerful, healing love. As I have gradually accepted the plan God has for me, and His love, my fears and confusion are slowly being replaced with hope for a better future. I'm learning patience and waiting in expectation for the picture of my life, as God envisions it.

The greatest discovery of my journey is that God continually chooses flawed, messed up, failing individuals to carry out his goals. People like Moses, Abraham, Noah, Gideon, David, Peter, John, Paul (yes, even you and I) have been selected by God to do great things. Every person listed above has made mistakes, failed to be perfect, and some have done unspeakable things. We're all damaged and yet God chooses us. In fact, His love is the greatest love in all the universe and God wants us to share this with everyone who is willing to listen.

So, my final prayer for you is this: That your life will be forever changed because of my book, and may your journey never end.

Reviewing this Chapter

Is there anything in your life that is preventing you from having a deep relationship with God?

_____

_____

_____

_____

_____

_____

_____

What do you believe you need to do in order to overcome these obstacles?

_____

_____

_____

_____

_____

_____

_____

Has your life been puzzling or difficult?

_____

_____

_____

_____

_____

_____

_____

_____

What are you willing to do to change your circumstances and find hope?

_____

_____

_____

_____

_____

_____

_____

_____

Epilogue

Wrapping Things Up

Do you feel this book has been beneficial in your life? My struggles with depression nearly caused me to end my life, but I discovered hope through seeking God. I still find my nemesis Satan and depression trying to take root in my life, but I cling on to this Bible verse from Zechariah 3:2 (GNT):

> *"In the name of the Lord, I rebuke you Satan, for I am branded for God and was plucked from the fires of hell!"*

I would love to have you share your experience with me so we can celebrate together. Please email me and share what has occurred in your life because of this book. I want to hear from you.

God-seekers@davidharder.com

You will find references for the following scriptures in this book. Here is a summary of those scriptures:

Second Timothy 3:16 (Good News Translation – GNT)

"All Scripture is inspired by God and is useful for teaching the truth, rebuking error, correcting faults, and giving instruction for right living."

Luke 23:43 (GNT)

"I promise you that today you will be in Paradise (heaven) with me."

Numbers 22:28–30 (GNT)

"Then God gave the donkey the power of speech, and it said to Balaam, 'What have I done to you? Why have you beaten me these three times?' Balaam answered, 'Because you have made a fool of me! If I had a sword, I would kill you.' The donkey replied, 'Am I, not the same donkey on which you have ridden all your life? Have I ever treated you like this before?' 'No,' he answered."

Jeremiah 29:11–13 (New King James – NKJ)

"For I know the thoughts I think toward you, says the Lord, thoughts of peace and not of evil, to give you a future and a hope. Then you will call on Me and go and pray to Me, and I will listen to you. And you will seek Me and find Me, when you search for Me with all your heart."

Acts 13:22 (NKJ)

"He (God) raised up for them David as king, to whom also He (God) gave testimony and said, 'I have found David the son of Jesse, a man after My own heart, who will do all My will.'"

Psalm 23 (GNT)

"The Lord is my shepherd; I have everything I need. He lets me rest in fields of green grass and leads me to quiet pools of fresh water. He gives me new strength. He guides me in the right paths as he has promised. Even if, I go through the deepest darkness, I will not be afraid, Lord, for you are with me. Your shepherd's rod and staff protect me. You prepare a banquet for me, where all my enemies can see me; you welcome me as an honored guest and fill my cup to the brim. I know that your goodness and love will be with me all my life, and your house will be my home as long as I live."

Psalm 37:8 (GNT)

"Don't give in to worry or anger; it only leads to trouble."

Proverbs 14:29(GNT)

"If you stay calm, you are wise, but if you have a hot temper, you only show how stupid you are."

James 1:19(GNT)

"Remember this, my dear friends! Everyone must be quick to listen, but slow to speak and slow to become angry."

Jeremiah 29:11–13 (NKJ)

"For I know the thoughts I think toward you, says the Lord, thoughts of peace and not of evil, to give you a future and a hope. Then you will call on Me and go and pray to Me, and I will listen to you. And you will seek Me and find Me, when you search for Me with all your heart."

Romans 3:23 (GNT)

"Everyone has sinned and is faraway from God's saving presence."

Romans 6:23 (New Living Translation – NLT)

"For the wages (or payment) of sin is death, but the gift of God is eternal life through Christ Jesus our Lord."

Matthew 19:25–26 (GNT)

"The disciples were astounded. 'Then who in the world can be saved?' They asked. Jesus looked at them intently and said, 'Humanly speaking, it is impossible. But with God everything is possible.'"

Romans 10:9–10 (GNT)

"If you confess that Jesus is Lord and believe that God raised him from death, you will be saved. For it is by our faith that we are put right with God; it is by our confession that we are saved."

Hebrews 11:1 (GNT)

"To have faith is to be sure of the things we hope for, to be certain of the things we cannot see."

Luke 22:31–32 (GNT)

"Simon, Simon! Listen! Satan has received permission to test all of you, to separate the good from the bad as a farmer separates the wheat from the chaff. But I have prayed for you, Simon, that your faith will not fail. And when you turn back to Me, you must strengthen your brothers."

Romans 8:34 (GNT)

"Who, then, will condemn them? (The sinners of this world) Not Christ Jesus, who died, or rather, who was raised to life and is at the right side of God, pleading (communicating) with Him (God) for us!"

John 17:20 (NKJ)

"I do not pray for these alone, but also for those who will believe in Me through their (the followers of Jesus) word; that they all may be one, as You, Father, are in Me, and I in You; that they also may be one in Us, the world may believe that You sent Me."

Numbers 23:19 (NLT)

"God is not a man that He should lie. He is not a human that He should change his mind. Has He ever spoken and failed to act? Has He ever promised and not carried it through?"

Exodus 21:23–25 (NKJ)

"But if any harm follows, then you shall give life for life, eye for eye, tooth for tooth, hand for hand, foot for foot, burn for burn, wound for wound, stripe for stripe."

Leviticus 24:17–18 (GNT)

"Any who commit murder shall be put to death, and any who kill an animal belonging to someone else must replace it."

John 8:7–9 (GNT)

"As they stood there asking Him questions, He straightened up and said to them, 'Whichever one of you has committed no sin may throw the first stone at her.' Then He bent again and wrote on the ground. When they heard this, they all left, one by one, the older ones first. Jesus was left alone, with the woman still standing there."

John 8:10–11 (GNT)

"He (Jesus) straightened up and said to her, 'Where are they? Is there no one left to condemn you?' 'No one, sir,' she answered. 'Well, then,' Jesus said, 'I do not condemn you either. Go, but do not sin again.'"

Luke 6:41 (NKJ)

"And why do you look at the speck in your brother's eye, but do not perceive the plank in your own eye?"

Romans 12:19–21 (GNT)

"Never take revenge, my friends, but instead let God's anger do it. For the scripture (Old Testament) says, 'I will take revenge, I will pay back, says the Lord.' Instead, as the scripture says: 'If your enemies are hungry, feed them; if they are thirsty, give them a drink; for by doing this you will

make them burn with shame.' Do not let evil defeat you; instead, conquer evil with good."

John 5:16–18 (GNT)

"So they began to persecute Jesus, because he had done this healing on a Sabbath. Jesus answered them, 'My Father (referring to God) is always working, and I too must work.' This saying made the Jewish authorities all the more determined to kill him; not only had he broken the Sabbath law, but he had said that God was his own Father and in this way had made himself equal to God."

John 10:30 (GNT)

"The Father and I are one."

John 3:16 (GNT)

"For God loved the world so much that He gave His only Son (Jesus), so everyone who believes in Him may not die but have eternal life."

Matthew 24:42–44 (GNT)

"Watch out, then, because you do not know what day your Lord will come. If the owner of a house knew the time when the thief would come, you can be sure that he would stay awake and not let the thief break into his house. So then, you also must always be ready, because the Son of Man (Jesus) will come at an hour when you are not expecting him."

Luke 21:11 (NLT)

"There will be great earthquakes, and there will be famines and epidemics in many lands, and there will be terrifying things and great miraculous signs in the heavens."

Second Timothy 3:1–5 (NLT)

"You should also know this, Timothy, that in the last days there will be difficult times. For people will love only themselves and their money. They will be boastful and proud, scoffing at God, disobedient to their parents, and ungrateful. They will consider nothing sacred. They will be unloving and unforgiving; they will slander others and have no self-control; they

will be cruel and have no interest in what is good. They will betray their friends, be reckless, be puffed up with pride, and love pleasure rather than God. They will act as if they are religious, but they will reject the power that could make them godly. You must stay away from people like that."

Second Peter 3:10 (GNT)

"But the Day of the Lord will come like a thief. On that Day the heavens will disappear with a shrill noise, the heavenly bodies will burn up and be destroyed, and the earth with everything in it will vanish."

Ephesians 6:12 (NLT)

"For we are not fighting against people made of flesh and blood, but against the evil rulers and authorities of the unseen world, against those mighty powers of darkness who rule this world, and against wicked spirits in the heavenly realms."

Second Corinthians 4:4 (NLT)

"Satan, the god of this evil world, has blinded the minds of those who don't believe, so they are unable to see the glorious light of the Good News that is shining upon them. They don't understand the message we preach about the glory of Christ, who is the exact likeness of God."

Second Corinthians 11:13–15 (NLT)

"These people are false apostles. They have fooled you by disguising them-selves as apostles of Jesus. But I am not surprised! Even Satan can disguise himself as an angel of light. So it is no wonder his servants can also do it by pretending to be godly ministers. In the end, they will get every punishment their wicked deeds deserve."

Psalms 1:1–6 (GNT)

"Happy are those who reject the advice of evil people, who do not follow the example of sinners or join those who have no use for God. Instead, they find joy in obeying the Law of the Lord, and they study it day and night. They are like trees that grow beside a stream, that bear fruit at the right time, and whose leaves do not dry up. They succeed in everything they do. But evil people are not like this at all; they are like straw the

wind blows away. Sinners will be condemned by God and kept apart from God's own people. The righteous are guided and protected by the Lord, but the evil are on the way to their doom."

John 4:1–26 (GNT)

"You are right when you say you don't have a husband. You have been married to five men, and the man you live with now is not your husband. You have told me the truth."

Luke 6:41 (NKJ)

"And why do you look at the speck in your brother's eye, but do not perceive the plank in your own eye?"

Galatians 6:1–5 (GNT)

"My friends, if someone is caught in any wrongdoing, those of you who are spiritual should set him right; but you must do it in a gentle way. And keep an eye on yourselves, so you will not be tempted, too. Help carry one another's burdens, and in this way you will obey the law of Christ. If you think you are something when you are nothing, you are only deceiving yourself. You should each judge your own conduct. If it is good, then you can be proud of what you yourself have done, without having to compare it with what someone else has done. For each of you have to carry your own load."

James 1:12–13 (GNT)

"Happy are those who remain faithful under trials, because when they succeed in passing such a test, they will receive as their reward the life which God has promised to those who love him. If we are tempted by such trials, we must not say, 'This temptation comes from God.' For God cannot be tempted by evil, and he tempts no one."

Luke 18:22–25 (GNT)

"'There is still one more thing you need to do. Sell all you have and give the money to the poor, and you will have riches in heaven; then come and follow me.' But when the man heard this, he became sad, because he was rich. Jesus saw that he was sad and said, 'How hard it is for rich people

to enter the Kingdom of God! It is much harder for a rich person to enter the Kingdom of God than for a camel to go through the eye of a needle.'"

Jonah 1:1–3 (GNT)

"One day the Lord spoke to Jonah son of Amittai. He said, 'Go to Nineveh, that great city, and speak out against it; I am aware of how wicked its people are.' Jonah, however, set out in the opposite direction to get away from the Lord. He went to Joppa, where he found a ship about to go to Spain. He paid his fare and went aboard with the crew to sail to Spain, where he would be away from the Lord."

Jonah 1:9–17 (GNT)

"'I am a Hebrew,' Jonah answered. 'I worship the Lord, the God of heaven, who made land and sea.' Jonah went on to tell them that he was running away from the Lord. The sailors were terrified, and said to him, 'That was an awful thing to do!' The storm was getting worse all the time, so the sailors asked him, 'What should we do to you to stop the storm?' Jonah answered, 'Throw me into the sea, and it will calm down. I know it is my fault that you are caught in this violent storm.' Instead, the sailors tried to get the ship to shore, rowing with all their might. But the storm was becoming worse and worse, and they got nowhere. So they cried out to the Lord, 'O Lord, we pray, don't punish us with death for taking this man's life! You, O Lord, are responsible for all this; it is your doing.' Then they picked Jonah up and threw him into the sea, and it calmed down at once. This made the sailors so afraid of the Lord that they offered a sacrifice and promised to serve him. At the Lord's command a large fish swallowed Jonah, and he was inside the fish for three days and three nights."

Isaiah 40:28–31 (GNT)

"Don't you know? Haven't you heard? The Lord is the everlasting God; he created all the world. He never grows tired or weary. No one understands his thoughts. He strengthens those who are weak and tired. Even those who are young grow weak; young people can fall exhausted. But those who trust in the Lord for help will find their strength renewed. They will rise on wings like eagles; they will run and not get weary; they will walk and not grow weak."

Ezekiel 28:12–17 (GNT)

"You were once an example of perfection. How wise and handsome you were! You lived-in Eden, the garden of God, and wore gems of every kind: rubies and diamonds; topaz, beryl, carnelian, and jasper; sapphires, emeralds, and garnets. You had ornaments of gold. They were made for you on the day you were created. I put a terrifying angel there to guard you. You lived on my holy mountain (heaven) and walked among sparkling gems. Your conduct was perfect from the day you were created until you began to do evil. You were busy buying and selling, and this led you to violence and sin. So I forced you to leave my holy mountain, and the angel who guarded you drove you away from the sparkling gems. You were proud of being handsome, and your fame made you act like a fool. Because of this, I hurled you to the ground and left you as a warning to other kings."

Second Corinthians 11:14 (GNT)

"Well, no wonder! Even Satan can disguise himself to look like an angel of light!"

Genesis 3:14 (GNT)

"Then the Lord God said to the snake, 'You will be punished for this; you alone of all the animals must bear this curse: From now on you will crawl on your belly, and you will have to eat dust as long as you live.'"

Matthew 4:3–10 (GNT)

"Then the Devil came to him (Jesus) and said, 'If you are God's Son, order these stones to turn into bread.' But Jesus answered, 'The scripture says, "Human beings cannot live on bread alone, but need every word that God speaks."' Then the Devil took Jesus to Jerusalem, the Holy City, set him on the highest point of the Temple, and said to him, 'If you are God's Son, throw yourself down, for the scripture says, "God will give orders to his angels about you; they will hold you up with their hands, so not even your feet will be hurt on the stones."' Jesus answered, 'But the scripture also says, "Do not put the Lord your God to the test."' Then the Devil took Jesus to a high mountain and showed him all the kingdoms

of the world in all their greatness. 'All this I will give you,' the Devil said, 'if you kneel down and worship me.' Then Jesus answered, 'Go away, Satan! The scripture says, "Worship the Lord your God and serve only him!"'

Luke 4:13 (GNT)

"When the Devil finished tempting Jesus in every way, he left him for a while."

Matthew 28:20 (GNT)

"And I will be with you always..."

Hebrews 13:5 (GNT)

"I will never leave you; I will never abandon you."

Romans 8:38–39 (GNT)

"For I am certain that nothing can separate us from God's love: neither death nor life, neither angels nor other heavenly rulers or powers, neither the present nor the future, neither the world above nor the world below – there is nothing in all creation that will ever be able to separate us from the love of God which is ours through Christ Jesus our Lord."

Psalm 23:1–6 (GNT)

"The Lord is my shepherd; I have everything I need. He lets me rest in fields of green grass and leads me to quiet pools of fresh water. He gives me new strength. He guides me in the right paths, as He has promised. Even if I go through the deepest darkness, I will not be afraid, Lord, for you are with me. Your shepherd's rod and staff protect me. You prepare a banquet for me, where all my enemies can see me; You welcome me as an honored guest and fill my cup to the brim. I know that Your goodness and love will be with me all my life; and Your house will be my home as long as I live."

Luke 6:47–49 (GNT)

"Anyone who comes to Me and listens to My words and obeys them – I will show you what he is like. He is like a man who, in building his house, dug deep and laid the foundation on rock. The river flooded and hit

that house but could not shake it, because it was well-built. But anyone who hears My words and does not obey them is like a man who built his house without laying a foundation; when the flood hit that house it fell at once – and what a terrible crash that was!"

Philippians 3:8 (GNT)

"...I reckon everything as complete loss for the sake of what is so much more valuable, the knowledge of Christ Jesus my Lord. For his sake I have thrown everything away; I consider it all as mere garbage..."

Malachi 3:10 (GNT)

"Bring the full amount of your tithes to the church... Put me to the test and you will see that I will open the windows of heaven and pour out on you in abundance all kinds of good things."

Joel 2:25–26 (GNT)

"I will give you back what you lost in the years when swarms of locusts ate your crops. It was I, who sent this army against you. Now you will have plenty to eat, and be satisfied. You will praise the Lord your God, who has done wonderful things for you."

Matthew 6:33 (GNT)

"Instead, be concerned above everything else with the Kingdom of God and with what he requires of you, and he will provide you with all these other things."

Zechariah 3:2 (GNT)

"In the name of the Lord, I rebuke you Satan, for I am branded for God and was plucked from the fires of hell!"

BIBLE SOURCES

Scripture quotations marked (NKJ) and scripture taken from the New King James Version®. Copyright © 1982 by Thomas Nelson, Inc. Used by permission. All rights reserved.

Scripture quotations marked (NLT) are taken from the Holy Bible, New Living Translation, copyright © 1996, 2004, 2007 by Tyndale House

You will find references for the following prayers in this book. Here is a summary of those prayers:

Chapter One

God, I am asking You to hear these words being read. Send Angels to watch over and protect me. I'm feeling depressed and hopeless, or can't make sense of life, but I am willing to read this book. Help me to understand, and push all preconceived ideas out of my head.

Chapter Two

God, I am asking You to hear these words being read. Send Angels to watch over and protect me. I feel depressed and hopeless, and can't make sense of life, but I want to know You. Help me to understand the words of the Bible and push all the negative thoughts out of my head.

Chapter Five

God, thank You for hearing the words I'm reading. Thank You for sending Angels to watch over and protect me. I feel angry and frustrated, and honestly don't like my life up to this point, but I want to know the truth about You. Help me to understand the words of the Bible and focus on how much You care about me.

Chapter Six

God, thank You for hearing the words I'm reading. Thank You for sending Angels to watch over and protect me. Thank You for praying for me, even though I didn't know it. I'm getting to know who You are, and I'm ready to enter the door of truth. I want to know more. Forgive me for my self-ishness, my failures, and for not including You in my life. Help me to understand faith and hope. Open new doors of truth for me so I may know even more about You.

Chapter Seven

God, thank You for hearing the words I'm reading. Thank You for sending Angels to watch over and protect me. Thank You for dying for me and praying for me, even though I didn't know it. I'm glad You are in my life because You have forgiven me for my selfishness and failures. I'm ready to continue forward and have You open new doors of truth for me. Give me wisdom so I can understand what I read in the Bible.

Chapter Eight

God, thank You for hearing the words I'm reading. Thank You for sending Your Angels to watch over and protect me. I'm glad You are in my life because You have forgiven me for my failures. You are opening new doors of truth for me and providing wisdom so I can understand what I read in the Bible. Teach me how to pray, and provide me with other God-seekers, like myself, to join me on my journey for the truth. Protect me from anything evil and grant me wisdom to decide who is evil or good. I want to continue seeking You and I love You, because You first loved me.

Chapter Nine

God, thank You for hearing the words I'm reading. Thank You for placing Your Angels around to watch and protect me. Teach me to love and forgive other people, because You love and have forgiven me. You are in my life and I rejoice. Thank you for Your wisdom and answering my prayers. Protect me from the enemy and do not let him rob me from You. I will continue to seek You because I am reading Your words and they will guide me on my journey for truth.

Chapter Eleven

God, I know you listen to me when I pray and are delighted in my words. Your name and love are greater than anything I can think of.

You've given me Angels to watch and protect me, because I give my mind, body, and soul to You. I hold nothing back from You. I may be capable of earning a living, buying food, and running my life, but every moment of my life I want to remember that I am Your creation, and You provided these things for me in the first place. I forgive those who have hurt me so I can receive forgiveness from You. Teach me to love people who injure me. Protect me from the enemy Satan and do not let him rob me from You. I know that I am now part of You and I will tell You everyday how happy this makes me. The earth and the stars will eventually be destroyed, but You and Your heaven will last forever. Amen

References

1 http://*miss-jkim.hubpages.com*

2 http://www.drjoecarver.com/clients/49355/File/DEPRESSION-Causes,Symptoms,andTreatment.html

3 http://cnsnews.com/news/article/447-million-americans-now-food-stamps-more-any-time-under-bush

4 http://www.drugabuse.gov/publications/drugfacts/nationwide-trends

5 http://www.cdc.gov/nchs/fastats/divorce.htm

6 http://en.wikipedia.org/wiki/Religious_views_of_Charles_Darwin

7 http://www.huffingtonpost.com/2013/03/21/universe-age-planck-space-probe-date-big-bang_n_2922818.html

8 http://englishmajorsunite.com/2012/07/03/the-ten-most-published-books-in-the-world-3/

9 The Bible, Good News Translation, Luke 23:32–43

10 The Bible, Good News Translation, Numbers 22:21–41

11 The Bible, The New King James Version, II Samuel 11:1–21

12 The Bible, The New King James Version, II Samuel 12:1–23

13 The Bible, The Good News Translation, Luke 22:39–46, Matthew 26:36–46, and Mark 14:32–42

14 http://en.wikipedia.org/wiki/Hematidrosis

15 The Bible, The New King James Version, Matthew 4:18–20 & 16:18, Mark 1:16–18, and Luke 5:1–11

16 The Bible, The New King James Version, Matthew 26:31, Mark 14:26–31, Luke 22:34, 39, and John 13:37–38

17 The Bible, The New King James Version, Matthew 26:69–75, Mark 14:66–72, Luke 22:56–62, and John 18:15–18, 25–27.

18 http://en.wikipedia.org/wiki/S%26H_Green_Stamps and http://en.wikipedia.org/wiki/Blue_Chip_Stamps

19 www.groupon.com/

20 The Bible, The New King James Version, Ephesians 1:7

21 http://en.wikipedia.org/wiki/Duncan_MacDougall_(doctor)

22 The Bible, The Good News Translation, Luke 23:39–43

23 The Bible, The New King James Version, Luke 22:54–62

24 The Bible, The New King James Version, Jeremiah 29:11–13

25 The Bible, The New King James Version, Luke 6:12–19 and Mark 3:13–19

26 The Bible, The Good News Translation, John 20:24–29

27 The Bible, The New King James Version, Luke 24:44–48

28 The Bible, The New International Version, John 17:19–26

29 http://www.deathpenaltyinfo.org/history-death-penalty

30 The Bible, The New King James Version, John 8:1–11

31 http://www.biblestudytools.com/history/flavius-josephus/

32 The Bible, The New King James Version, Matthew 28:9–10, 16–20, Mark 16:9–20, Luke 24:13–53, and John 20:11–29

33 http://en.wikipedia.org/wiki/Parable

34 The Bible, The Good News Translation, Luke 3:23

35 http://www.neverthirsty.org/pp/corner/read1/r00307.html

36 The Bible, The New King James Version, Mark 16:19, Luke 24:49–53, and Acts 1:9

37 The Bible, The Good News Translation, Matthew 25:31–46

38 http://www.sacred-texts.com/bib/boe/boe009.htm, http://www.sacred-texts.com/bib/boe/boe010.htm, and http://www.sacred-texts.com/bib/boe/boe011.htm

39 *Star Wars.* Written and directed by George Lucus. 1977. Marin, CA: 20th Century Fox, 2004. DVD.

40 The Bible, The New King James Version, Genesis 3:1–5

41 The Bible, The New King James Version, Genesis 3:17–24

42 The Bible, The Good News Translation, Revelation 20:1–3, 10

43 *Star Wars.* (see reference 39. above)

44 *Avatar.* Written and directed by James Cameron. 2009. London, UK: 20th Century Fox, 2010. DVD.

45 *Terminator.* Directed by James Cameron. 1984. Los Angeles, CA: Orion Pictures, 1997. DVD.

46 *Independence Day.* Directed by Roland Emmerich. 1996. Los Angeles, CA: 20th Century Fox, 2000. DVD.

47 *Men in Black*. Directed by Barry Sonnenfeld. 1997. Los Angeles, CA: Columbia Pictures, 2012. DVD.

48 *Mork & Mindy*. First broadcast 14 September 1978 by ABC. Executive producers Anthony W. Marshall and Garry Marshall.

49 *Third Rock*. First broadcast 9 January 1996 by NBC. Executive producers Bonnie Turner and Terry Turner.

50 *X-Files*. First broadcast 10 September 1993 by Fox. Executive producers Chris Carter and R. W. Goodwin.

51 http://www.cbsnews.com/8301-501465_162-20017713-501465/united-nations-appointing-ambassador-to-alien-world/

52 http://theeconomiccollapseblog.com/archives/who-owns-the-media-the-6-monolithic-corporations-that-control-almost-everything-we-watch-hear-and-read

53 http://www.wtop.com/681/2920761/People-believe-in-aliens-survey-finds

54 http://www.aufosg.com/index.php?option=com_content&task=view&id=55

55 The Bible, The Good News Translation, John 4:17–18

56 *Terminator*. (see reference 45. above)

57 The Bible, The New Living Translation, Psalms 103:12

58 The Bible, The Good News Translation, Luke 11:1

59 http://www.ncdc.noaa.gov/extremeevents/specialreports/Hurricane-Katrina.pdf

About the Author

David Harder is currently residing in the White Mountains of Arizona. In addition to writing, he is a clay artist whose work is featured in Lark Books, "500 Pitchers." He also uses his art in a form of ministry. By using clay and a potter's wheel, he demonstrates in churches and presents a message correlating God as the potter and we humans as the clay. This is a powerful, scripture-based message that infuses David's personal testimony with a physical presentation.

He grew up in southern California and served in the US Navy during the Vietnam conflict. For nearly eight years, he lived and worked in Germany and traveled many countries throughout Europe. Upon returning to America, David settled in northern California working for many Silicon Valley start-up companies. Starting out in sales and marketing, he eventually became a CEO and business owner before retiring and moving to Arizona in 2006.

A graduate of San Jose College with a degree in business, David also studied at Santa Clara University towards a degree in international business. During his career in the computer industry, he has traveled all over the world. Most of his career centered on companies with cutting-edge computer and storage technologies.

To schedule David for a clay presentation, or to purchase additional copies of *Carving Hope Out of Depression*, you may reach him through his website at www.DavidHarder.com

CPSIA information can be obtained
at www.ICGtesting.com
Printed in the USA
FSOW02n0300160216
16960FS